# 101 GREAT MONEY MAKING IDEAS

**MARK HEMPSHELL**

# 101
# Great
# Money
# Making
# Ideas

'Opportunity is everywhere.'
— *Charles Clore*

**Northcote House**

**Publisher's Note**

Readers of this book — which is intended primarily as a handbook of ideas and opportunities — are cautioned to seek proper professional advice before making important business or financial decisions and this book is not in any way to be considered a substitute for such advice. Readers are reminded that business law and regulations are liable to change.

**British Library Cataloguing in Publication Data**
Hempshell, M.
    101 great money-making ideas.
    1. Business enterprise. Success, –
Proposals
I. Title
650.1

ISBN 0-7463-0536-2 (PB)
ISBN 0-7463-0540-0 (HB)

First published in 1989 by Northcote House Publishers Ltd, Harper & Row House, Estover Road, Plymouth PL6 7PZ, United Kingdom. Tel: Plymouth (0752) 705251. Fax: (0752) 777603. Telex: 45635.

Typeset by Peregrine Typesetting, Perranporth, Cornwall.
Printed and bound in Great Britain by
Richard Clay Ltd, Bungay, Suffolk

# CONTENTS

*Preface*                                                          9

*Introduction*                                                    11

**Fact File**                                                     13

**Project File 1: Out & About Businesses**
 1 Adult Education                                                32
 2 Leaflet Distribution                                           34
 3 Estate Agency                                                  37
 4 Commercial Property, Land & Business Sales                     40
 5 Mind-A-Home Service                                            41
 6 Auctions                                                       43
 7 A Concert or Play                                              46
 8 A Dance or Disco                                               49
 9 Demonstration Selling                                          50
10 A Shop Within a Shop                                           53
11 A Seasonal Shop                                                53
12 Clearance Sale                                                 56
13 Mobile Video Library                                           57
14 Gift Wrapping                                                  58
15 Gift Delivery                                                  60
16 Sign Supply                                                    61
17 Advanced Driving Tuition                                       63
18 Other Driving Techniques                                       65
19 Tour Guide                                                     65
20 Flower Selling                                                 67
21 Selling Fads                                                   69
22 Special Interest Weekends                                      71
23 A Van Sales Round                                              73

# Contents

24 A Press Agency 75

**Project File 2: Office & Desk Businesses**
25 Opportunities in International Trade 80
26 Property Renovations 83
27 Property Decoration 86
28 Finance Broker's Agent 86
29 Other Financial Services 89
30 Market Research 90
31 Telephone Market Research 93
32 Advertising Cards 94
33 Dealing in Surplus Stock 96
34 Credit Control 98
35 House Exchange 101
36 Souvenir Plots of Land 103
37 A Dating Agency 105
38 A Contact Service 107
39 Company Sales Agent 109
40 Telephone Services 111
41 A Mailing List Broker 113
42 Editing & Proofreading 116
43 A Car Broker 118
44 A Used Car Broker 120
45 A Free Newspaper 121
46 A Mini-Advertising Agency 124
47 Tours & Excursions 127
48 Party Organisation 130
49 Art Sales 132
50 Barter 134

**Project File 3: Practical Businesses**
51 Replacement Kitchen Doors & Drawers 138
52 Home Improvements 141
53 Telephone Fitting 142
54 Foil Printing 144
55 Natural Cosmetics 145
56 Natural Foods 147
57 Biscuits 148
58 A Sandwich Service 150
59 Street Catering 152
60 Making Food for Restaurants 153
61 Bulk Breaking 156
62 Picture Framing 157
63 Repairing & Refurbishing 159

*Contents*

64 Second-hand Furniture 161
65 Reupholstery 162
66 Contract Maintenance 164
67 Equipment Cleaning 167
68 A Laundry Service 170
69 Car Valeting 172
70 Alarm Installation 174

**Project File 4: Creative & Artistic Businesses**
71 Writing About Your Interests 178
72 Travel Writing 180
73 Writing Verse for Greetings Cards 182
74 Calligraphy 184
75 Video Film Production 186
76 School Photography 187
77 Street Photography 190
78 A Postcard Photo Library 192
79 A Complete Photo Library 194
80 Plant Rental 195
81 Interior Design 196
82 Jewellery Making 199
83 Junk Jewellery 202
84 Ideas for Games 202

**Project File 5: Self-Managing Businesses**
85 Door-to-Door Catalogue Sales 206
86 Mail Order 208
87 A Business Services Bureau 209
88 A Computer Bureau 210
89 A Printer's Jobber 212
90 Picture Rental 214
91 Subdividing Office Space 215
92 Subdividing Shop Space 218
93 A Courier Service 219
94 Sandwich Board Advertising 221
95 A Language School 222
96 A Translation Service 225
97 Fancy Dress Hire 226
98 Vending Machines 228
99 Public Conveniences 230
100 Other Coin-operated Facilities 232
101 Lotteries 233

**Resource File** 235

# PREFACE

'Everybody has the skill to launch, develop and succeed in a business project of their own!'

This claim was recently made by a successful entrepreneur, a fan of the 'start from scratch' business opportunity. It may sound unrealistic, but his statement is perfectly valid. A small project can be started with modest capital, taking up little time. It may not need complicated skills, yet it is as capable of growing as any larger venture.

What most beginners lack is ideas — sound ideas supported by the facts essential for success. That is where this book comes in. I have put together a wide range of ideas for making money, some part-time, others full-time, some requiring a significant amount of capital, others virtually none at all. More and more people are discovering that they have the capacity to branch out on their own. I aim to show you what is possible. After that, it's up to you. If you have the interest and the drive, and if you have chosen your project carefully, you will succeed.

Anyone can benefit from this book, whatever their qualifications, skills or previous experience, provided they also have the most important ingredient of all — determination. Whether you are already in business, a full-time employee or unemployed, you have the skills to succeed — here are the ideas and information to help you.

*Mark Hempshell*

# INTRODUCTION

I have tried to make this collection of ideas as imaginative and varied as possible. About the only thing the projects have in common is that they are all suitable as 'starter' businesses: businesses that are easy to establish, but will show a prompt return. Some are small sideline ideas, others have 'tycoon' potential. Some are ideal for owner-operators, others require staff. Some are 'temporary' businesses, for operation when you need the money; others will continue for many years. Some are full-time, others part-time. Some need special knowledge or skills, others none. And the **Fact File** at the beginning of the book provides general guidance on setting up your business.

The projects are grouped into broad categories — Out and About, Office and Desk, Practical, Creative and Artistic, and Self-Managing — but obviously there are some ideas which could fall into more than one category. Street photography, for example, requires you to be out and about, but it is also a creative activity. Where this kind of overlap occurs, I have opted for the category which seems most appropriate.

Each project starts with a few basic facts about the idea: the *status* (part-time or full-time); the *capital required* (high or low); the *return* (whether high or low in relation to the capital required, and whether you will show a profit in the long or short term); and any *other projects* with which it could be combined. Usually no more than two other projects are given in this category, since you are unlikely to want, or be able, to operate more than three businesses at one time. A few, however, can be combined with more. The projects themselves are organised so as to make it easy for you to follow from one stage to the next — what you need before you start, the pros and cons of that particular business, how to run it, how much you can expect to make out of it.

I would suggest that you use the following step-by-step plan for assessing which ideas will be most suitable for you.

1. Read the projects, one by one.
2. Make a note of those that interest you.
3. Make a shortlist of about five or ten, and try to place them in order of preference.
4. Consider how they could be adapted to your circumstances.
5. Prepare a short written appraisal, assessing each project, particularly with regard to the capital, time and resources needed, and your estimated return within a certain time.
6. Cut this shortlist down to the three likeliest projects. It should then be possible to choose the most attractive one, keeping the others in reserve.
7. Research your chosen project thoroughly. Read up on it. Look at any permission or licences you need, prices and availability of supplies, potential customers, the amount of administration needed and your ability to cope with it, staff needs, and of course its financial viability given your circumstances.
8. If at this stage, you have any doubts, choose one of your 'reserves', and analyse that — or try something totally different. If your research shows that you can do it, then get started!

Finally, although I have taken all reasonable care to ensure that the details given in this book are correct, it is always advisable to check the current position for yourself. I would also strongly advise you to consult your professional advisers (accountant, bank manager, lawyer) at every stage.

Now you can move to stage 1 — and good luck!

# FACT FILE

Whatever kind of project you decide on, there are certain processes essential to setting up any new business.

## How to choose an opportunity
Your choice of business should be based on the following criteria.

1. **Time.** Some businesses need a regular daily commitment, others just a few hours occasionally.
2. **Money.** Some businesses can start without much capital, others need several thousand pounds. Mostly, the greater your investment the faster the business becomes viable and the larger it will be.
3. **Resources.** Some opportunities need a fully equipped office and staff. Others are owner-operated from home.
4. **Status.** Some opportunities are only suitable for part-time operation. Others must be full-time. Some offer a choice.
5. **Term.** Some opportunities offer a fast return, others produce profits in months or years rather than weeks.

## Planning your venture
Questions to ask yourself when planning your venture:

- What **input** is required, in terms of money, time etc?
- What do I need to **start** (e.g. a telephone, a series of advertisements in the local press)?
- Where do I get the **supplies** I need to run my business? Can I get reliable supplies at the right price?
- Who are my **customers?** Do they exist in sufficient numbers in my business area?

- Can I sell my **product** or **service** effectively? By what method?
- Roughly, what are my sales likely to be? Can I **test** this in some small way before starting in business proper?
- Even assuming the worst **sales figures,** are sales likely to be worth my while and what I consider to be the minimum needed?

## Forming a company

In the UK you don't need permission to start in business in a general way. Any individual or group of people is allowed to trade as a business.

People trading on their own account are considered **sole traders.** A sole trader has full personal liability for his business and any debts incurred, but also has full control over the concern.

Individuals trading together are known as a **partnership.** Here the liabilities and control are shared. A partnership agreement (made through a solicitor) is advisable and this should lay down how disputes between partners are to be resolved.

Those starting in business may apply for limited liability status. The **limited company** is a legal body which offers owners limited liability against some debts. The Registrar of Companies, Crown Way, Maindy, Cardiff, CF4 3UZ, is the place to register, but an accountant can handle the procedure.

Most new businesses start out on a sole trader or partnership basis, but you should get the advice of a solicitor and an accountant. Some advise that company status is only worth having where turnover is expected to exceed £100,000, but this is not always the case.

## Choosing a business name

All businesses should choose a trading name. This might be your own name or a special business name. In the UK there is no need to **register** a name, nor any central register of names to consult, except for limited companies.

One **legal requirement** is that the name you choose should not be the same as one already in use. A superficial check can be made through telephone directories. Names may not include terms such as 'National' which implies national ownership. If the name used is not the owner's name then your name and official business address (even if it is your home) must be displayed on business documents, and at the business premises by means of a small but prominent notice.

A booklet (C469) advising on choice of company business names

PARTICULARS OF OWNERSHIP OF:

_____ (Name of Business)

As required by the Companies Act 1981 (section 29)

Full name of the Proprietor(s) and their Address(es) in Great Britain at which documents may be effectively served is/are:

_____

_____

_____

_____

(List names of owners and official business address)

Example of a notice giving particulars of ownership of a business trading under a business name.

is available from the Registrar of Companies.

## Licences and permission
No general business licence is required in the UK, but a few businesses may need **official permission** because of the nature of the products and services they sell. For example, businesses handling food require environmental health clearance from the local council.

The best course of action is to check licence needs with a solicitor or business adviser before starting any business. If licences are needed the local council is usually the appropriate body, but it could be HM Customs & Excise or some other public authority.

## Raising finance
These are the main ways of raising finance, in order of preference:

- **Own** capital and savings.
- Capital borrowed (possibly interest free) from **friends and relatives.**
- A loan from a **bank or financial institution.**

It is sometimes possible to get outside **investors** to inject capital in a business venture in return for a share of the profits. Look for 'venture capital available' advertisements in newspapers. Before borrowing money in this or any other way consult an accountant and a solicitor.

## Banking

As soon as capital is available arrange separate banking facilities to handle the **business finances.** It is usually practical to do your business banking at the same branch as your personal banking. The main exception is when specialist financial transactions occur, for example, in import-export. For this a major city branch is a must. Ask your bank manager for an introduction to a new bank if necessary.

Banks will apply **charges** to business accounts (unlike most personal ones). Get written details. Managers may negotiate a reduced or no-charge period for new business customers.

It can be useful to open up a line of credit by way of an **overdraft.** Again, charges could be negotiable. For an overdraft you may have to pay an arrangement fee, in addition to interest. Security may be required (such as a first or second mortgage on your house).

## Taxation and National Insurance

All income is liable to **tax.** The Inland Revenue have a booklet (IR28) giving basic details. It contains a form you can use to advise them that you have started in business. The address of your local office can be found under **Inland Revenue** in the telephone directory.

If you are full-time self-employed you will pay tax by annual assessment. If you are a limited company you will draw a monthly payment (salary), subject to Pay-as-You-Earn (PAYE) taxation.

If you are part-time self-employed, perhaps with a full-time job, make this clear to the Inland Revenue.

It will pay you to consult an accountant at the outset, and ideally retain him to deal with all taxation matters.

**National Insurance contributions** are payable by those in business, except for very small part-time earnings. Ask the Department of Social Security for booklets NP15, NP18, NI27A, NI41, N208. For your local office look under **Social Security** in the telephone directory.

## Value Added Tax

This is a tax payable on sales by businesses with a turnover above a certain limit. Such businesses can also reclaim the tax they pay on most purchases. **Registration** once you reach the limit is compulsory; below the limit it is voluntary.

Ask HM Customs & Excise for the booklet *Should I be Registered for VAT?* and the current registration limit. For your local office, look under **Customs & Excise** in the telephone directory. If in doubt as to whether to register they will advise impartially, or you can consult an accountant.

## Insurance

At the outset consult at least three insurance brokers. Tell them of your plans and ask them to advise and quote for any compulsory and any useful but non-compulsory insurance.

**Motor insurance** is a well-known requirement, but a special policy may be needed for business use of vehicles. If you operate from premises, both **buildings** and **contents insurance** may be required. **Public liability insurance** (should a customer be injured on your premises) is advisable. It is also possible to insure for **product liability** (should injury be caused by a faulty product or service). You should also consider permanent health insurance, covering loss of income due to illness.

## Working from home

Working from home is a good, low-cost way of testing a new idea. Strictly speaking though, residential properties do not have **planning consent** for business use. While a discreet business, like one conducted by telephone, rarely causes trouble you do officially need 'change of use' planning consent for anything more.

If working from home check with:

- the local council planning department to see if you need any planning consent
- your building society, if the property is mortgaged
- your landlord, if the property is rented
- your insurance company to clear insurance problems
- a solicitor, to check house deeds for restrictive covenants
- your neighbours, to head off possible disputes!

## Working from premises

By their very nature some businesses (shops, for instance) need special premises. In others, premises are optional but provide many benefits over home operations, such as extra space and 'site' advertising. However, premises-based businesses do require a higher capital investment.

Go through the following checks when looking for premises:

1.  Take your accountant's advice on **renting** or **buying.**
2.  Find out the **going rate** for the type of premises you require.
3.  Use **commercial estate agents** to find a property for you.
4.  Don't agree to lease or purchase without a **valuation** and **survey** from a surveyor and advice from a solicitor.
5.  Make sure you have 6 months' rent (or mortgage payments) in **cash** before starting, plus capital to cover insurance, rates, electricity and water, and decoration and furnishing costs.
6.  For **flexibility,** don't lease for more than 5 years.

### Setting up an office

You should take time to set up an office. Whether you are using a spare bedroom or a prestige suite you will probably need some if not all of the following:

*   A **telephone** — contact British Telecom for a system appropriate to your needs.
*   A **typewriter** if possible an electronic one. You could buy one second hand via classified ads. Or you could use a typing service.
*   Access to **services** like photocopying and word processing, and possibly even telex and fax. (You could retain a business services bureau.)
*   **Files** — ring binders and lever arch files for storing documents and to act as ledgers.
*   At least one **filing cabinet.**
*   **Stationery** — every business needs letterheads and business cards. Instant print shops can be costly, so look for a printer in the Yellow Pages. Use one who handles commercial printing as this will be a good contact for sales literature.

Smart office fittings should only be bought where they will be seen by customers. Otherwise buy from second-hand dealers and use surplus capital in the business, for advertising and so on.

### Routine administration and accounts

All businesses need a good **accounting system,** no matter how small the turnover. Ask an accountant to advise you on an appropriate method for your business. Or use a book-keeping service or part-time book-keeper.

If you handle the books yourself one of the standard accounts books (available from commercial stationers) should suffice. Alternatively keep three basic files — Sales, Purchases and Bank Payments. These should be totalled monthly. Support them with the invoices and receipts you have issued to customers or obtained from suppliers.

I would strongly advise anyone setting up a new business to use an accountant, if only to prepare the annual accounts which will be needed for taxation purposes.

## Employing staff

Many new businesses are owner-operated. But some will require staff. If you are unfamiliar with **personnel matters** always take professional advice on recruiting. A Job Centre will help with free vacancy advertising and recruiting in most cases. For executive positions retain a recruitment agency on commission. Look under **Employment Agencies and Consultants** in the Yellow Pages.

Discuss **employment legislation** with a solicitor. Until you have a clear idea of your needs, it may be better to offer staff temporary contracts rather than permanent, even though this makes recruitment harder.

Consult the Inland Revenue and Department of Social Security and tell them you are becoming an **employer.** You will have to collect tax and contributions from your employees. You can sometimes avoid this administrative work by using self-employed subcontractors or keeping wages below the current taxation limit.

## Legal advice

All new businesses should take legal advice. It is best to arrange a preliminary consultation with a **solicitor** to discuss plans and open up contact in case you need legal advice in the future. Approach three or four and go for the one you feel is most interested in small businesses.

Your solicitor should have some knowledge of **commercial law.** This usually means a town or city practice. If your business has special needs, for example, where property transactions are involved, be sure they can also be met.

Some businesses involve unique legal aspects. If you are at all legally minded you can check on particular facts for yourself. Use a reference guide like *Chitty – Statutes,* which is kept at most major reference libraries.

## Accounting

Before starting your business, you should take advice from an **accountant.** Choose one suited to your type and size of business, and one who deals with both business and personal matters. Personal recommendation is the best way of finding one, or you can approach those who advertise. Your bank manager will sometimes recommend one.

The first job for an accountant is to advise on a book-keeping system. The second is to prepare the financial information you need to run the business — including annual accounts.

Give details of your accountant to the Inland Revenue and your bank. Then if they need information they can go straight to the accountant. Always consult your accountant on your financial plans and aims. He can advise and spot problems at an early stage.

## How to deal with suppliers

All businesses have suppliers, whether it is the printer of your letterheads, or the manufacturer of the product you sell. For those not used to dealing with suppliers a few tips might help.

It is important to realise that most suppliers **want** new customers, even small buyers. No matter how new or small your business, don't underestimate your value to a supplier. Give a professional image and they will be interested in doing business.

When choosing suppliers the general rule is to track down at least three and ask them to **quote** for your needs. The Yellow Pages are always the first place to look for suppliers in a trade of which you have no prior knowledge.

Dealing with suppliers usually involves **negotiating** in some way. Rarely pay 'list price' without negotiating first. A good way of operating is to put your requirements out to tender. This makes it clear to suppliers that you are asking others for quotations and they must be competitive (see sample letter opposite).

Try to make personal contact with suppliers. Go to see them or ask their **representative** to call. In this way, you can often negotiate reductions on their initial price.

Once you have several quotes for supplies cost them carefully to ensure that they fit your plans and **budget.** Don't order until you are convinced.

When **ordering,** get all details in writing, not only price, but also quantity, type of product, delivery and payment terms. Subsequent problems can ruin the profitability of your project. It is good business practice to use a standard order form for all orders (see page 22).

**THE ABC COMPANY LIMITED**
22 The High Street, Anytown. Tel. 123456

**TENDER REQUEST**

To:　Jones & Smith Printers
　　　The Industrial Park
　　　Anytown

Dear Sirs
<u>Brochure Printing</u>
We would be pleased to receive your most competitive tender for printing of our new Winter 19— Brochure and Price List. The brochure consists of approximately 20 pages, printed both sides. Each set of pages should then be bound with either a spiral ring or a heat-bonding system.
Specifications : We require offset litho quality printing, black plus 2 standard colours on white A4 size 80 gsm paper. Your price to include typesetting and production of artwork from our typewritten lists, all printing, finishing, binding and delivery to the above address.
We would require the work completed within 30 days from date of order, and would also require a further 30 days' standard trade terms payment facility.
2,500 copies of the brochure will be required.
Please submit your quotation for the work not later than 20 July 19—. If you are unable to tender for our requirements please let us know.
Yours faithfully


J.R. Jones
Sales Manager

Enclosures : We enclose a copy of a competitor's brochure, the quality of which must be matched by ours. Also enclosed is a copy of our draft brochure/price list to illustrate the subject matter.

Specimen letter asking for a tender.

## SMITH'S PHOTOGRAPHY SERVICES
1 Grange Avenue, Townford. Tel.987654.

### ORDER

*Order Number:* 1          *Date:* 22.7.—
*Order to:*          The Townford News,
                     Press Buildings,
                     Cheapside, Townford.

*Please Supply:*

10 Full Display advertisements in your 'Services' column
on each of 10 subsequent Fridays starting 29.7.—.
Size of advertisements to be 2 columns wide by 10
centimetres deep — a total of 20 single column centimetres
at £3.00 per s.c.m.

All as agreed during our telephone conversation of today's
date with your Mr. Wright, ie the advertisement will be the
first inserted in the 'Services' column each week. Copy for
this advertisment is attached. We understand all artwork is
included in your price.

*Payment Details:*

End of month following your invoice. Or we may deduct
5% discount for payment within 7 days.


Signed, for Smith's Photography Services :   ....   J. Smith.

Specimen Order

Finally, most suppliers are used to handling all sorts of enquiries, so you don't have to be 'in the trade' to canvass them with a view to starting a business based on their products.

## How to make business contacts

The same principles apply in making business contacts as in locating suppliers. In other words, most people in business are interested in making more business contacts. So create and develop your own growing network of contacts and colleagues.

**Personal** contacts are useful for many purposes. Whether you

---

Cedar Cottage
Upper Burton
Cambridge

**TO WHOM IT MAY CONCERN**
Re:     Mr John Smith

I have pleasure in confirming that I have known Mr John Smith for approximately 8 years, during his part-time employment by my wife and myself as a ............. .

Now that I have retired from my business I have no hesitation in recommending Mr Smith to any associate with whom he may seek to deal in the course of his new business.

At all times I have found him to be honest and reliable in his dealings. During my years in my business of ...........
his contribution was a considerable benefit to the business. I was able to leave him in sole charge on many occasions.

I am able to vouch for the fact that Mr Smith has carefully thought out his new business plans, and feel that any supplier he approaches can deal with him in confidence.

Yours faithfully,


J. Basil

---

Specimen letter of recommendation from an existing
business contact

need an accountant, a solicitor or a good printer it can be much easier going to a personal contact rather than canvassing totally new companies.

An excellent way of making contact is by referral and **recommendation** by someone you already know. On a more formal basis, written **references**, like the example on the previous page, are often a good way of getting contacts. If you have established business contacts, you could ask them for a letter recommending you to others and perhaps noting your satisfactory business record with them. If you do not have any existing contacts look for them from advertisements in the press or the Yellow Pages. A simple letter introducing yourself could be enough to make a valuable contact for future use. It is a useful method of getting your name known to anyone, and anywhere.

---

### S. WILLIAMS INTERIOR DESIGN
The Cottage, Anyvillage, Berkshire.
Tel: 234567

Dear Sir

A NEW SERVICE — AVAILABLE FROM 1st AUGUST!

I should like to introduce my new professional interior design service, available from 1st August.

We offer a full service to domestic and smaller commercial clients in expert design and specifying of decor and furnishings. Quite simply, we are able to take an empty room and transform it with imaginative, thoughtful design — and subsequently arrange all necessary work.

If our service is of interest please telephone to arrange a preliminary consultation. There is no fee for our initial survey and advice.

Yours faithfully

Sandra Williams

---

A specimen letter introducing your business to prospective clients. It is not a sales letter as such, but it gets your name known.

Good quality business notepaper and quality typing is a vital requirement for any business letter, especially the introductory ones.

## How to get credit

Generally, most suppliers are very willing to give new customers **credit.** Never offer payment without asking for the standard 30 days' credit. If payment has to be made in advance a **discount** of 2½% – 5% should be requested.

A simple letter requesting credit can be sent to all new suppliers (see the example on page 26). State your business address, names of owners and references. These should include a bank and two trade suppliers (if you don't have any suppliers yet, give the name of your accountant or anyone who has given you credit in the past).

On receipt of an application which is professional in approach the majority of suppliers will grant credit, or at least seriously consider it. If a supplier does not offer this standard business facility it may be better to buy elsewhere.

When applying for credit, estimate the amount of credit you can afford and take care not to exceed it.

## How to advertise

No business can exist without advertising in some form. There are surprisingly few different types, but an important business skill is to identify the best forms of advertising for your particular project.

**Newspapers and magazines.** These are always the first choice for advertising. Local and regional newspapers are cost-effective and easy to use, though only suitable for local and regional businesses. National publications can be expensive, so are only suitable for products and services you can sell nationally. You should also consider specialist media relating to your specific business. *Benn's Media Directory* and similar guides, which are available at libraries, list all the publications you can use. Ask each for a rate card. Most newspapers have specialist sales staff who will help you.

**Yellow Pages.** This is a must for all new regular businesses as it prompts unsolicited enquiries, and one advertisement lasts a full year. Generally, take the largest space your budget will allow, possibly advertising in more than one section. There are other similar local directories. They are quite expensive, but very cost-effective. They are only published annually, so reserve space in the next issue as soon as you start.

---

**ABC SERVICES**
1 The Close, Anytown. Tel. 567890


Browns Wholesalers Ltd                 22.7.—
The Trading Estate
Anytown

Dear Sirs

Application to Open a Credit Account

We refer to your Summer 19— Catalogue recently received and have pleasure in confirming our intention to place business with your company. Will you please therefore open a credit account in the name of ABC Services. Please consider the following standard credit information:

Name & Address: ABC Services, 1 The Close, Anytown.
Name & Address of Proprietor: Mr Graham Jones, address as above.
Amount of credit required: £2,500 maximum.
Credit terms: All sums due will be paid at the end of month following your offical invoice (or 30 days standard trade terms).
Bankers: Barclays Bank plc, High St, Anytown.
Trade References:
1. J.B. Hawkins & Co  (Accountants), High St Anytown.
2. Marsh Printers Ltd, Townford Rd, Townford.

Should you require further information please do not hesitate to let us know. Alternatively, please confirm acceptance of our application at the earliest convenience so that we may place our initial orders.

Yours faithfully


G. Jones
Proprietor

---

A specimen letter requesting credit

**TV and radio.** These are rarely used, as they are quite expensive. TV is only for major projects but is suited to some regional businesses. Radio is more localised, but really is only suitable for certain types of well-known products or services. It is best to consult an advertising agency for advice.

**Leaflets.** These are suitable for local 'town-wide' businesses. They are a good, cheap way of launching a new business quickly. Consult a specialist printer and leaflet distributor.

**Mailshots.** This is a good advertising method when you are selling to other businesses (not so good when selling to the public). Names can be taken from telephone directories and an attractive mailing piece sent out. It can be expensive, so is only suitable for products and services of high value (£100 or more). Consult a specialist writer and/or mailing agency for advice.

**Direct canvassing.** Personal or telephone calls on prospective customers should be considered an advertising technique. Direct canvassing is suitable for both trade and retail customers (e.g. door-to-door selling). It is very cheap, though sometimes a great deal of 'cold canvassing' has to be done to get some worthwhile prospects. There are marketing agencies or freelance representatives who will do this sort of work, sometimes on commission.

**Buses, hoardings etc.** Advertising on buses and hoardings can be a good method for local businesses, though it is really only suitable as a supplement to other techniques. Consult the local bus company or the agency for hoardings as shown on the hoarding itself.

**Other methods.** There are other methods of advertising, but they should be considered as minor and only suitable to support major methods. Use them only when you have surplus advertising capital from the major methods. Advertising on local guides, street maps, parking meters and sandwich boards can be worthwhile. But test their potential as it relates to your particular business first.

Advertising agencies can look after your entire advertising requirements for a particular project for a set fee. Find one in the Yellow Pages (look under **Advertising Agencies**). However, most agencies will only be interested in a certain annual turnover of advertising business so may not be of help to smaller concerns.

If you want or need to do your own advertising *The Creative Handbook* is an essential publication. It gives contacts for consultants, designers, illustrators, printers, publishers etc. you can use to produce professional advertising material. It is published by Thomas Skinner Directories, and is available at major libraries.

## How to sell

Selling is a distinct operation from advertising. Advertising gets a business lead, your sales effort converts it into income.

Selling is a mixture of customer **information, explanation** and **persuasion.** Any business owner with commitment usually makes an excellent salesperson, even if they do not consider themselves good at selling. The following tips will help:

- Be well informed on your product or service.
- Get to know competing products or services.
- Always have professional sales literature to hand, whether manufacturers' brochures or your own.
- Prepare a sales presentation for the customer.
- Don't hesitate to meet the customer person to person, but always make an appointment first.
- Explain the nature of the product fully. If you mention both advantages and disadvantages it goes down well.
- Tell the customer what the product or service can do for them.
- If possible, offer sale-or-return terms or a free sample.

Considerable effort should be made to get initial sales. These can be used as 'testers' for future sales efforts.

A great deal of **canvassing** can be done initially by mail. This breaks the ice and makes personal selling easier. Assume, for example, that you have identified a possible new customer and want to approach them to offer your services. A well-written letter could be valuable in creating a sales opportunity (see next page).

If you really don't feel you can sell personally then employ sales staff. Advertise through Job Centres or in the 'sales staff' column of the newspapers.

## Writing business letters

Despite increasing use of telecommunications in business, **letter-writing** is still a useful skill. It can have great value in getting new business contacts and in selling. The following tips will be useful for those unused to business letters:

- Good business stationery and a typewriter are essential.
- Always quote the name and address of the person you're writing to at the top of the letter.
- Start 'Dear Sir' or 'Dear Mr ...', as appropriate.

- Most letters should have a heading for quick reference explaining the subject to be discussed.
- The first paragraph should always refer to any previous contact.
- The second paragraph should launch immediately into the subject. Ask clearly for what you want.
- Keep any non-essential information very brief.
- The final paragraph should instruct the reader what to do next.
- After the final paragraph finish with 'Yours sincerely' after 'Dear Mr ...', or 'Yours faithfully' after 'Dear Sir', and nothing else. Always sign letters personally and type your name and/or position underneath.

---

**COUNTY ADVERTISING COMPANY**
Specialists in Advertising Card Publishing
10 The Grove, Anytown. Tel: 123123

Dear Sirs

We should like to introduce ourselves as publishers of high-impact advertising cards — a revolutionary new advertising concept.

This technique involves publication of an attractive, durable card which is circulated door-to-door in areas targeted as successful for your business. The card, carrying a professionally designed advertisement for your business, is generally retained — and used — by about 75% of the householders who receive it.

This represents an outstanding but economic advertising opportunity. We would very much like to visit you at a convenient time to explain the proposition and suggest the sort of results it could create for you.

Our representative will telephone you in the next few days to ascertain if we are able to help you further.

Yours faithfully


G.J. Brown

---

A specimen letter canvassing for business

- Add a 'PS' to highlight important items, especially in a sales letter.
- Keep it concise — no more than one page if possible.

## Operating several businesses

There is no reason why you should not operate several businesses together. Many business people do. Most of the projects in this book are ideal for joint operation.

It would be wise, however, to ensure **compatibility**. Check the following points:

1. **Capital.** Adequate investment must be available for all projects.
2. **Time.** Ensure sufficient time is available for everything.
3. **Resources.** Can your office space and staff cope without your having to buy in extra resources which could make the extra project unviable?
4. **Conflicts.** Is there a conflict of interest? You should not usually, for example, both sell and hire tools and equipment.
5. **Supplier problems.** How will suppliers take to sidelines? For example, a baker's shop supplying bread for your sandwich service may not be pleased if you start a competing shop nearby.

## Getting further help

There are many sources of further help in business. Often it is free. A list of useful addresses appears at the end of the book but here are some you should consult as a matter of course:

**Small Firms Service.** Operated by the Department of Trade and Industry it offers (initially free) business advice. Dial 100 and ask the Operator for Freefone 2444.

**Training Commission.** Offers training (and sometimes finance) for small businesses. Contact via Job Centres.

**Business in the Community.** A useful enterprise agency for local help. Tel.01-253 3716.

**Local councils.** Many have a Business Officer or a Development Agency. They can help in dealing with regulations, finding premises and sometimes finance.

**COSIRA (Council for Small Industries in Rural Areas).** Can help with advice in country or small towns. Tel.(0722) 336255.

**Banks.** Useful financial advice and guidance on the possible viability of a new project.

# PROJECT FILE 1
# Out and About Businesses

This chapter consists of businesses which are
not confined to an office or workshop, but which
involve going out, travelling and meeting people.
For this reason they can be attractive to many
people who dislike the idea of being confined to
their office or home. Conversely, some people,
such as mothers of small children, might find them
difficult to undertake.

## PROJECT 1: ADULT EDUCATION

| | |
|---|---|
| *Status* | Part-time, full-time later |
| *Capital required* | Low |
| *Return* | High, short-term |
| *Can be combined with* | Projects 19 and 95 |

### Project facts

Additional education is a readily saleable product! It is not always necessary to have any great skills to be able to teach others. Quite simply, if you have an ordinary day-to-day skill, it can be sold to others as a course or evening class.

What may seem to be mundane skills to you can have enormous commercial potential. For example, a good amateur car mechanic, a home knitter, even a keen house-plant grower, could all offer their skills as a lucrative course.

### What do I need?

- A saleable skill.
- Possibly a licence — check with the local authority.
- A venue. A school is ideal, as it will be well equipped — ask the secretaries of your local schools. Otherwise hire a hall (look under **Halls** in the Yellow Pages). You could even run small classes in your home.
- The journals *Education* and *Training and Education* may help in structuring a course.

### Pros and cons

**Pros**
Minimal outlay
No delay in payment
Can be arranged to
fit in with other
activities

**Cons**
Needs a lot of preparation
Difficult to estimate demand
in advance

### How do I operate?

Decide on the skill you will offer, and work out a course. A typical course might consist of six 1½ hour lessons, each covering an aspect of the subject. Try to make the lessons as interesting and varied as possible. Each lesson might include a talk, audio-visual material and practical work.

Find a venue. Your Local Education Authority or further education college might be interested in offering your course, or else might be able to advise you on suitable venues. Arrange a suitable time. Evenings usually suit most people.

Having put your course together and arranged a time and place, you will need to advertise. Local newspapers and shop windows are the best places to advertise this sort of thing.

You can either ask students to pay for the whole course in advance at the first lesson, or get them to pay for one lesson at a time.

Your first course will always be the most difficult, but once the content is established, it will be easy to duplicate it over several courses, or several years. In time you could diversify into other subjects, and even open a full-time school for more popular subjects, like secretarial skills.

Alternatively, you could work as a part-time lecturer for an existing college. This will save you some administrative work, and will resolve any doubts you may have about whether there will be sufficient demand, but you will probably earn less than you would on your own.

## How much can I earn?

Fee income can be considerable, but varies according to the subject. Fees will be higher for courses that are not readily available cheaply at local evening classes.

**Example:** An experienced calligrapher arranged a beginners' course in calligraphy covering all aspects over six weekly lessons. Each lesson lasted two hours.

The fee charged for the course was £55 (payable in weekly instalments) and 22 students enrolled, bringing in a total income of £1,210. The only substantial cost was the hire of a classroom at a college — £8 per session, plus about £100 to advertise the course in the local press.

The organiser was therefore making over £1,000 profit for the complete course. This could perhaps be repeated three times a year, and in a further three venues in the same region.

## Summary
1. Decide whether you have a skill you can teach.
2. Check whether you need a licence.
3. Prepare a course.
4. Find a venue and arrange a time.
5. Advertise in the press and in shop windows.

# PROJECT 2: LEAFLET DISTRIBUTION

| | |
|---|---|
| *Status* | Part-time, full-time later |
| *Capital required* | Very low |
| *Return* | Moderate in short term |
| *Can be combined with* | Projects 32 and 89 |

## Project facts

One of the most effective, cost-efficient ways of promoting a product is the distribution of leaflets from door to door. Such a technique offers an advertiser considerable advertising space, but at a low cost per leaflet — an arrangement that can rarely be bettered by press advertising, directories and the like.

Unfortunately, there are few properly organised leaflet distribution companies who can offer a first-rate service, so there is room for beginners to open up, with the incentive that those companies who do distribute in an effective way can develop to a considerable size.

## What do I need?

- A telephone and some storage space at home.
- A car or van to transport leaflets and droppers.
- A team of leaflet droppers. Advertise in shop windows for part-time droppers and offer around £2 – £3 per hour.
- The journals *Campaign* and *Marketing* may contain information of interest.

## Pros and Cons

| Pros | Cons |
|---|---|
| Minimal outlay | Requires organisational and supervisory skills |
| Once established, can be expanded fairly easily | Some clients may need convincing of the value of the service |
| Employs others to do the work! | |

## How do I operate?

The first thing to do is to recruit customers. This also lets you test demand. To make one leaflet drop pay you will need at least three different businesses whose leaflets can be dropped together — five if at all possible. Many firms already use promotional leaflets, many more could be persuaded to do so.

Leaflet users include small local firms and large national ones who drop leaflets and special offers nationwide. Public authorities also sometimes use leaflets. Any business whose product can be promoted by leaflet is a potential customer. The Yellow Pages is a good source of names. Telephoning potential users is the best sales technique, or you can write to them. Remember to sell not just your service, but the concept of leaflets as advertising too.

Continue with your selling until you have a profitable number of customers and leaflets to drop. Try to get contracts for regular drops each month or so. You might, for example, get 30,000 to drop for a local shop, 50,000 for a local supermarket, 50,000 for, say, a chocolate bar manufacturer and 20,000 for the local council. Always bulk them together for a profitable drop.

Most customers will supply you with ready-printed leaflets, although you can organise design, copywriting and printing for them for an extra charge. It is your prime job to ensure effective distribution.

As I have said, the best way to drop leaflets is to employ part-time droppers, paid hourly. Advertise for them locally. The best droppers are housewives, active pensioners and students. Give each a brief interview to determine their suitability and reliability then put them on your droppers' register. An active firm will probably need about twenty part-time droppers.

Droppers must work on their own initiative. You provide the leaflets and transport and leave them to get on with it. One important task however is to plan drop zones. To do this, buy Ordnance Survey maps of your area. Identify major areas of housing. Visit these areas yourself — determine their status, e.g. wealthy, middle-class, working-class areas. Estimate roughly the number of homes in each of the major areas and write these details on your map.

Careful work here allows you to match products on leaflets with the areas most suited to them. This will get the best response for your customer and further work for you. A leaflet on replacement windows, for example, might not go down well in an area of mainly council housing, but could be very successful in an estate of modest private houses built prior to 1970 where existing windows might need replacement.

Use your map and local knowledge to plan routes for each distributor. Give each distributor approximately the right number of each leaflet and notes on the route to cover. Drop them off and pick them up as necessary.

You need not become too concerned with the actual dropping, except to see that it is carried out effectively. Most distributors have a system of spot checks on droppers' work. Do this yourself or employ supervisors to plan routes and check up on small teams of five droppers each.

Report back to your customers when the drop is complete and keep in touch with them throughout the subsequent response period. The response they obtain will give valuable information on that area as a future target, and perhaps ensure that you get lucrative repeat orders from your clients.

## How much can I earn?

Leaflets are a progressive form of communication used by many big companies. Distributing them offers income far in excess of what might be expected.

**Example:** A typical charge for delivering 1,000 leaflets might be £18 — not a great deal by itself. But consider that a good distributor might deliver up to five leaflets in the same drop. Your income is now effectively £90 per 1,000 'letter-boxes visited' — £900 per 10,000 — £9,000 per 100,000 or £90,000 per 1,000,000!

Good droppers can drop 1,000 in a day, earning perhaps £20. So, on 1,000 the organiser's profit is £70 — on 1,000,000 — £70,000!

Distribution is very much a matter of clear, systematic organisation. If you can organise a drop of 50,000 leaflets for £750, you can organise one of 50,000,000 (over a longer period of course) for £750,000! So just continue to expand your area (there is potential to operate nationally) and attract larger and larger customers.

## Summary
1. Investigate and set rates before starting.
2. Always drop several leaflets per round. One will not pay.
3. Aim to get regular contracts wherever possible.
4. Research target areas personally, and thoroughly.
5. Use part-time distributors as much as possible.

# PROJECT 3: ESTATE AGENCY

| | |
|---|---|
| *Status* | Full-time |
| *Capital required* | High |
| *Return* | Good, long-term. |
| *Can be combined with* | Project 26 |

## Project facts

Experts suggest that the value of estate agency work will grow to £3,000 billion within 10 years, and that existing agents will not be able to absorb it all.

Market research also suggests that existing agents are keen to specialise in up-market properties, so there are openings for newcomers to offer budget services from an agency started at minimum cost and dealing in low-priced properties. A lower level of know-how is needed for such a budget business than is normally associated with estate agency.

## What do I need?

- Capital or financing to support a business in the first year when costs are likely to exceed revenue.
- Shop premises (purchased or leased) in a busy area.
- Knowledge of the local property market.
- The guidance of a qualified surveyor with local knowledge. He will be of help in several areas, particularly valuation. Advertise for a surveyor in the local press. One may be willing to work part-time as an adviser to a new business. The professional association is the Royal Institution of Chartered Surveyors, 12 Great George Street, London SW1P 3AD (Tel. 01-222 7000). Or you can retain a valuer for this work (a valuer can value but not necessarily survey). The Incorporated Society of Valuers and Estate Agents is at 3 Cadogan Gate, London SW1X 0AS (Tel. 01-235 2282).
- A solicitor should be retained for occasional queries.
- The National Association of Estate Agents, 21 Jury Street, Warwick CV34 4EH (Tel. (0926) 496800) have an information service (fee charged).
- The *Estates Gazette* (available at main libraries) is a professional journal and good, technical insight into the business. They also publish several books on the subject of estate agency and valuation. Their address is 151 Wardour Street, London W1V 4BN.

## Pros and cons

| Pros | Cons |
|---|---|
| Growing market sector | Larger than average capital outlay |
| High profitability for an efficient business | Takes time to establish respected name |
| Lower overheads may allow you to offer a lower commission rate to attract business | Competition from financial institutions |

## How do I operate?

A business like this centres around the creation of a 'shop'. This is an advertising focal point and a centre for the display of property particulars. The outlet should be equipped to display details, and staffed by an experienced receptionist. Estate agencies these days are run on a more relaxed, informal basis and so the ability to deal sympathetically with people and help with their requirements is probably even more useful than specialist property knowledge.

A sales negotiator could be employed, or you could do this part of the work yourself. The job of the negotiator is to advise prospective sellers (vendors) and put their properties up for sale, as well as conducting negotiations between parties once offers are received.

Professional qualifications are not needed to run an estate agency, but you should thoroughly plan the procedure by which properties, vendors and buyers are handled. Most agents work in a similar way and a great deal can be gleaned from monitoring their activities. Some time will elapse before receiving the first enquiries from potential vendors. During this time the business needs to be promoted extensively, mainly through the local press. Once customers do make contact the system might be:

1. Receive enquiry from potential customer.
2. Undertake free valuation for enquirer (use surveyor).
3. On instructions to proceed, measure up house and produce descriptive particulars. Illustrate with photograph.
4. Confirm your selling fee in writing. (This is a legal requirement.) Your fee should be competitive for the local area. Typically it would be 1½% of value, plus cost of ads, plus VAT (if applicable).
5. Erect signboard at property (made by local joiner/signwriter).
6. Advertise property in your weekly features in all local newspapers. Their advertising departments will advise on the

best methods.
7. Display particulars in the shop and make them available to callers.
8. Prospective purchasers can then contact vendors direct.

The level of service provided by agents varies, but they are typically now mostly promotion agents, rather than handling every aspect. Tailor your service to your fees. Evidence suggests there is room for a 'bare-bones' service at around 1% commission, which is less than the current fees of 1½%–2%. Find out what the local competition charges for (a) sole agency and (b) joint or multiple agency.

Having said this, most agents offer help with negotiations. That is, they receive offers from prospective buyers and transmit them to the vendors with professional advice. If you are unsure of the valuation use a retained surveyor to advise you.

Once the vendor accepts an offer the property becomes 'Sold Subject to Contract'. At this point the agent should refer both vendor and purchaser to their respective solicitors to complete the transaction. The agent is not normally involved.

## Summary

1. Although estate agency has rarely been considered a start-up activity before, no professional qualifications are needed, and there is no reason why a newcomer cannot start.
2. Promote your business extensively before you start.
3. It may help to charge competitive fees to attract business.
4. Plan your procedures carefully.
5. Compete with the larger financial institutions by offering a personal service in the lower price brackets.
6. You should retain a quantity surveyor or a valuer and a solicitor to advise you.
7. Offer a 'bare-bones' service (simply advertising and promoting the property) at a lower fee than other firms. You will find a ready market for your services.

# PROJECT 4: COMMERCIAL PROPERTY, LAND AND BUSINESS SALES

*Status*               Usually full-time
*Capital required*     High
*Return*               Good, long-term

## In brief
Estate agency is not restricted to the sale of domestic property. It can operate in many other fields on exactly the same basis, for example:

- Industrial and commercial property — offices, factories and shops (freehold and leasehold).
- Land sales — development or agricultural land (best operated in conjunction with the first service mentioned).
- Business sales — selling businesses as going concerns, rather than just premises.

The advantage with these types of operation is that they can be established rather more cheaply than estate agents. Usually they operate from small office premises rather than shops and they do not always require staff. In addition, there is usually less competition than in estate agency, particularly if you start at the smaller end of the market, for example, properties of less than £100,000 value.

Anyone wishing to start such a venture should follow a similar procedure to estate agency, retaining the same advisers, but making it quite clear you are covering anything but residential sales. One point is that, as you are not competing directly with them, estate agents may be willing to provide the surveying and valuing support you need at very modest cost.

Further details on how to proceed will be found in **Project 3.**

## Summary
1. Dealing in commercial property is generally less complicated than it seems to outsiders, so you can succeed by offering a straightforward and informal service.
2. Keep your service small when you start. The bigger property deals are dominated by the large established agents.
3. Consider operating only locally to start with so that you can stay within your depth as a newcomer.

## PROJECT 5: MIND-A-HOME SERVICE

| | |
|---|---|
| *Status* | Ideally part-time only |
| *Capital required* | Very low |
| *Return* | Quick but moderate |
| *Can be combined with* | Project 70 |

### Project facts
The increase in burglary and vandalism increases demand for effective security services. Security alarms are one idea, but there is now also a demand for something more individual. As a result, a new type of home patrol service is developing. Similar to guard patrols for commercial premises the new 'home-minder' facilities offer a watchful eye over a home when the owners are away, or feel in need of security.

### What do I need?
- A telephone.
- Transport.
- A small amount of capital for advertising and stationery (suggest £50 or so).
- Part-time help with patrols. To ensure confidentiality this is an ideal family business.
- *Burglary in a Dwelling* by Mike Maguire (Heinemann, 1982) covers security from a criminological viewpoint, and would be useful background reading.

### Pros and cons
| Pros | Cons |
|---|---|
| There is huge potential market | It may take time to build |
| Very little outlay | a respected name |
| | The business has a seasonal |
| | element |

### How do I operate?
Your service will involve patrolling homes for security purposes — checking doors, taking in mail, perhaps switching on lights at night, maybe even watering plants as a sideline. This aids both physical security and acts as a deterrent.

To operate successfully you need to set up a competent and confidential business. Operate under a professional-sounding business name, perhaps even from an accommodation address in a prestige area. Complete the image with an insurance policy to cover customers against damage or theft while you are looking after their homes. For this, consult an insurance broker.

It is a good idea to inform the police of your new service in order that their suspicions will not be aroused. They will also give you advice.

Advertise in local and regional newspapers, through cards in local shop windows, use door-to-door leaflets (very high quality ones), but don't use door-to-door calling for this type of service. Remember, the service is for householders who will be away on holiday or business or just out during the day, and also elderly and handicapped people who would appreciate a daily 'security call'.

Visit those who enquire about the service in person to discuss their requirements. Decide what sort of service they want. This might range from a check on doors and windows to looking after pets and tidying the garden. All these things help to make the house look occupied and less likely to attract intruders.

Quote a daily rate for your service. Customers then just need to phone you when they require the service. Bill them and collect accounts monthly. A daily external check might cost £3, a detailed security check £8 per day over say a two-week holiday.

Actually running this service is perhaps the easy part after getting your customers. The best thing to do is to organise customers for each day into a 'round' to be fitted between other commitments. Try to vary the time of day and the order of visits for the maximum deterrent effect.

What you actually do depends on your arrangement with each customer. You might simply check the outside of the property. Alternatively, if the owner gives you the key you can go inside daily, opening and closing curtains, turning lights on and off, leaving the TV on at certain times or feeding the cat! All this will make an empty home look lived in. One minding service checks isolated properties in a country area. It also operates a useful sideline messenger service. Another specialises in elderly people, employing a trained nurse part time, mostly paid for by relatives.

This type of idea can be used as the basis for a multitude of different services. So try and fit it to the demands of your local area and don't keep too strictly to the ideas here.

## How much can I earn?

Such a service may not seem to have a great deal of profit scope. But figures tend to prove otherwise. Assume that in a medium-sized town a security service gained customers for five £3 calls and two £8 calls in a day. That amounts to £31 daily, and £217 weekly. Such a service might take no more than eight to ten hours to operate.

The service could be five times busier in the peak periods for this service — the summer holidays. As business builds up over a longer period several people could be engaged to make the security checks.

## Summary

1. You will need a professional-sounding name, and your advertising literature should match the image you are trying to create.
2. You should inform the police about your plans.
3. Advertise in local newspapers and by leafleting, but don't promote your business by door-to-door calling.
4. Consult an insurance broker about cover for clients while you are looking after their property.
5. The services you offer could range from a superficial external daily check while clients are away to a daily call on elderly or handicapped people.

---

# PROJECT 6: AUCTIONS

| | |
|---|---|
| *Status* | Part-time, occasional |
| *Capital required* | Low |
| *Return* | High, fast |
| *Can be combined with* | Projects 11, 12 and 22 |

---

## Project facts

Retailing takes many forms. One of the most interesting from the organiser's point of view is the auction. It offers a chance to make money from a sale, but at the same time there is no stock commitment.

Auctions are well-accepted methods of buying and selling property, livestock, arts and antiques and the like. So the auction organiser has a method of selling that buyers already accept. Auctions are, however, less well-used for some other goods, and this is where the opportunities are.

Anyone can organise, promote and hold an auction, and make money for very little risk.

## What do I need?
- Capital to advertise an event (£100 or more).
- Good organisational skills.

## Pros and cons

| Pros | Cons |
|------|------|
| Very little risk | Needs heavy promotion |
| Possible high return | Only occasional income |
| Money collected immediately | |

## How do I operate?

An auction sale is a relatively simple event. But it does need careful and accurate organisation if it is to be successful for sellers — and successful for the organiser. Basically you will be providing a venue and an auctioneer and then inviting the public to sell.

A qualified auctioneer is vital in order that the sale can be run honestly and legally. You will need to track down a qualified person locally who is prepared to work on an occasional basis. Many estate agents, valuers and similar professionals are auctioneers although they do not usually use this skill. A local one might be prepared to help. Agree the auctioneer's fees in advance. The appropriate professional association is the Incorporated Society of Auctioneers and Valuers, 3 Cadogan Gate, London SW1X OAS (Tel. 01-235 2282).

The venue should be a large hall which is readily accessible to large numbers of people. Apart from this it should have good access for whatever goods are to be auctioned. Town and village halls are usually ideal. Look under **Halls** in the Yellow Pages. You may need to book it for up to three days to cover the sale and prior viewing days.

The next important point to decide on is the products you will sell. Try to stick to a category of items, rather than invite all-comers. It is probably best to stay away from the very specialist areas like livestock or fine arts.

Good products are those that will sell for between £30 and £500. They include general antiques and bric-a-brac, household effects, collectors' items such as coins, furniture and the like. At the other end of the market cars, tools and equipment, bankrupt and discontinued stocks all make good auction lines. Your choice of product line is an individual matter. Bear in mind local conditions

— and take the advice of your auctioneer.

When you have decided the type of goods you will sell and booked an auctioneer and a venue you can move on to promotion. This takes two forms.

1. **Promoting to sellers.** To make the event work you will need people to come and sell their unwanted items, whether they are traders selling unwanted stock, or householders selling surplus furniture. You need as many as possible. Sellers *will* be interested if you give them plenty of notice. Advertise your sale prominently in local newspapers, shop window posters and leaflets stuffed door-to-door in the area.
2. **Promoting to buyers.** For this, you need a second and different type of advertising, this time encouraging people to attend the auction as buyers. All the above methods can be used, but you must quite specifically invite *buyers* to attend, and not assume they will respond to the same invitation as sellers.

The organisation of the auction itself could take the following form:

1. Entries for sale should close 7 days prior to the event.
2. Put entries into numbered lots.
3. Print a catalogue of lots. The cover price of say £1 could give admission to the auction.
4. The day prior to the sale admit the lots and arrange them into a display.
5. On the morning of the sale open the hall for viewing.
6. Start the sale at say 1.30pm.
7. All goods should be removed and accounts settled by 6pm the same day.

The actual conduct of the sale will be the concern of the auctioneer, so do be guided by him. You will simply need to arrange for lots to be on show at the point of sale (if possible) and for all monies to be collected afterwards. Set up a cashier's desk for the purpose of collecting from buyers and paying out sellers.

## How much can I earn?

Profits can be very high, and are often directly related to the promotion. Income comes from two sources: admission charges, which at £1 a head could well be £1,200 at a good venue, including viewings, and commissions. As organiser you can charge a commission (or premium) to sellers, and possibly to buyers too. This might be 5% each, plus a lot entry fee to the seller. 300 lots at a £5 entry fee would produce £1,500. If £12,500 worth of goods were sold commission might be £1,250. The total income from the auction would then be £3,950, less expenses. This amount will vary with the goods involved. It could be less for a small 'starter' sale. It could be far more for a well-established, major event.

## Summary

As a business opening the auction sale offers a rather special opportunity and as an event it is well established in the business scene. Yet it is neglected as an opportunity in many respects and so there are opportunities to start an entirely new operation within an established activity.

1. Always use a qualified auctioneer.
2. Spend a lot on promotion.
3. Never sell any significant amount of your own goods. Events that appear to 'mock' genuine auctions can be illegal.
4. Choose goods to sell carefully. If necessary test potential with small sales first. Repeat those which prove popular.

---

## PROJECT 7: A CONCERT OR PLAY

| | |
|---|---|
| *Status* | Part-time, occasional |
| *Capital required* | Low |
| *Return* | Very high |
| *Can be combined with* | Project 101 |

---

### Project facts

One well-established way of making money is to produce a product once, and sell it over and over again to different customers, in the same way, for example, that a publisher publishes a book and sells many copies, at the same price, of one original.

An interesting way of using this idea is in the organisation of a concert, for example with a rock band or a brass band, or a play. If you can organise and bring together all the things that make a good show you can benefit from the multiple profits that this sort of event can generate.

### What do I need?

- A telephone and desk space (you can work from home).
- Capital at least to finance the booking of a hall and performers. Suggest £200 or more for a very small event.

- Your local library will have details of local amateur bands, orchestras, dramatic societies and venues.
- Useful reference books are: *The British Theatre Directory* and the *British Music Yearbook* (annuals available at main libraries).
- A useful periodical is *Stage and Television Today* (available at main libraries).
- For more serious theatre useful background can be found in *The Oxford Companion to the Theatre* edited by Phyllis Hartnoll, published by Oxford University Press.

## Pros and cons

| Pros | Cons |
|------|------|
| Possibility of considerable income from a single event | Long lead times — may need several months to plan |
| | Risk of failure to break even |

## How do I operate?

There are many types of event to choose from. The best way is to select one in which you are personally interested:

- A pop concert with a live band or bands.
- A brass band, orchestra or string quartet.
- A choir, or operatic society.
- A play.

You could even have a mixture of several different events.

The most important step is to select your performers. This can be done to suit your capital. Major artistes could cost several thousands of pounds, but on the other hand you might get a local band or theatre group for £50 or so. Whatever you spend here will be reflected in the ticket price.

Explain your event to the performers. Agree fees, which might be a flat rate, or a percentage of sales, or both. Once agreed it is the performers' responsibility to produce an entertainment you can sell. Take no part in that side yourself.

A venue will need to be booked for a mutually convenient date. This will need to be of a standing suitable for the event and the entertainers. A local band, for example, could be housed in a community centre, but a leading choral society might expect a small theatre or at least a good town hall. Look for a venue under **Halls** in the Yellow Pages. Discuss the event with the hall manager so that all needs can be catered for. Then put the performers in touch so that details can be finalised. You may have to pay for the venue in advance.

Promoting the event is your most important job. A major event should be placed in the hands of a marketing agency. Most minor events can be handled directly. Use all the methods available:

1. The theatre or hall. It should have poster space available to promote the event, as well as mentioning it in programmes for their other events. This service can be free, or you can negotiate a fee.
2. Local and regional press. Take out advertisements from eight weeks before the event right up to date of performance. Newspapers may also give a listing in an entertainments guide.
3. Radio and TV. This is more costly but a must for major events. Contact local independent TV and radio stations.
4. Posters. Local hoarding space may be available — contact agencies named on hoardings. Also try local bus companies.
5. Leaflets, dropped door-to-door or available at certain key venues, may be worthwhile. This method may also be a suitable way of advertising in surrounding towns.

Monitor advertising carefully. Increase it if results are poor to prevent a flop. Decrease it if results are good to increase profits.

With advertising underway the next job is to sell and issue tickets and collect revenue. A theatre or major hall will probably have a box office who will do this for you. Failing this you can ask for postal bookings, with payment, to your home. Post tickets to purchasers.

One good idea is to appoint shops in the area to sell your tickets. Travel agents, estate agents and music shops are especially good but many other shops might do this. All the better if they accept credit cards. Provide them with sales posters and pay a commission on sales (perhaps 15%).

Ticket prices very much depend on the event. £15 might not be unreasonable for the best seats at a provincial opera, play or orchestral performance. £5 is a minimum nowadays for any event. Be advised by the venue manager and the performers.

Sell tickets on a 'cash with booking' basis. This money can be banked and interest used to subsidise payments you have already made.

Monitor ticket sales and preparation of the performance carefully. Usually you will have booked facilities and be committed to proceed. In some circumstances, however, you can cancel and lose only part of a deposit if ticket sales fail. On a similar theme you may very well be inundated with bookings. Should this be the case try to arrange additional performances. These would probably require at least one month's notice, so you need to monitor bookings very closely.

On the day of the event you have very little to do, except perhaps arrange sales of the programme you have put together for extra income. After all, you have paid the theatre or hall to organise the facilities and the band or dramatic society for the performance. So just sit back and enjoy it!

Successful events can be repeated on a larger scale in the knowledge that they will be profitable. An event that is profitable in a small town hall could well be a huge success six months later in a premier theatre.

## Summary
1.  Choose an event in which you are interested yourself.
2.  Select your performers and negotiate a fee.
3.  Find a venue appropriate to the event. A local band might be fine in a community centre, a choir would need something better.
4.  You will need to promote heavily, and monitor the response.
5.  Tickets can be sold at the theatre, or by you by post.

## PROJECT 8: A DANCE OR DISCO

| | |
|---|---|
| *Status* | Part-time, occasional |
| *Capital required* | Low |
| *Return* | Good, fast |

## In brief
Concerts or plays are an excellent way of raising funds, but the same principle can be applied to another leisure event — a dance or disco. This has the advantage of being rather simpler to organise than a concert.

First, decide on some sort of theme for your dance. A disco for younger customers is preferable, while dancing to a band is ideal for the older generation. Try and make the event something that can be organised on a regular basis (i.e. not seasonal like a Christmas dance), since most of your profit is to be made in repeat trade.

Careful planning will be required in organising both a venue (anything from a village hall to a night club) and a band, or a disc jockey for a disco. Generally, it is far better to go for an 'up-market', expensive arrangement than a budget event.

Advertising and publicity can be a problem. Use the local press. This is what makes the organisation of a regular event more attractive — in time, you won't need to advertise.

The event itself should be as straightforward as possible, needing a minimum of supervision. The main aim is to collect the takings from which to pay the expenses. A well-organised event could cost £5 and attract 450 patrons (£2,250). Compare this to a 'budget' event at £2 attracting only 150 people (£300) for a pricing principle that applies to many business activities.

Further details on how to proceed will be found in **Project 7.**

## PROJECT 9: DEMONSTRATION SELLING

| | |
|---|---|
| *Status* | Part-time, occasional |
| *Capital required* | Moderate |
| *Return* | Fast. Very high. |
| *Can be combined with* | Projects 11, 12 and 15 |

### Project facts

Many a successful salesman has said that, 'If you demonstrate something you will sell it'. The truth often goes even further than this: if you demonstrate something properly you don't need to sell it — it will sell itself! So the demonstration theme lends itself to making money, often quite speedily. Put simply — find something to sell, demonstrate it, sell it!

One sales demonstration opportunity that deserves special attention is the in-store demonstration stand, where you demonstrate products on a stand in the corner of a busy shop. With a good product idea you need a minimum of resources, but could build enormous sales within a very short period. This is ideal for those who want to sell, but don't want to do the selling!

### What do I need?

● A novel product to demonstrate and sell on site. *Gifts International* is a monthly journal covering gift products. It is published by Benn Publications, Sovereign Way, Tonbridge, Kent TN9 1RW (Tel. (0732) 364422).

- A shop to sell in. *The Stores, Shops and Hypermarkets Directory* will help find one. It is available in main libraries.
- A sales pitch and sales speech.

## Pros and cons

| Pros | Cons |
| --- | --- |
| Fast return on your investment | Suitable, exciting stock may be difficult to find |
| Relatively easy to set up | Not everyone can do this kind of selling |

## How do I operate?

Products for a stand must be attractive so as to stimulate impulse buying. Make sure they are bright and colourful. It is best if they are new in design. They should not be available easily in the shops (if at all). Or, if they are, your price should be lower. The ideal price bracket is between £3 and £10.

Exclusive imported products do well on demo stands, as do home-made craft goods. Sometimes bankrupt stock and discontinued lines do well if the prices are rock bottom. Products include toys, games, fancy goods, gifts, exclusive food items, jewellery and fashion accessories. Gadgets, fads and gimmicks are good lines. So you might sell a 'miracle' cleaning tool or junk jewellery! Don't stick to these ideas too closely. Anything can be inexpensively tested.

Any shop you use must be busy. Your stand space must be in one of the busiest parts, ideally near a door. The busiest city centre shops can be used all week. Quieter ones are suitable only on Saturdays. The best shops include department stores, chain stores, supermarkets, general markets and modern shopping centres.

Attitudes to demo stands vary. Some shops won't consider them. Others are happy to take them, depending on your product. Contact the manager and find out. You will pay a set fee or a percentage of your takings. Pay a percentage for an untested product, a set fee for a known winner! Book your stand days in advance to ensure there are no conflicting stands.

Stock levels can be hard to estimate with untested products. Arrange with your supplier to take back unsold stock, then take as much stock as you can. One trader sold 350 £7 cosmetic gift sets in one day at a busy department store just before Christmas.

A stand should be bright and colourful with its own lighting and ideally a public address system. Have a counter for demonstrations, with shelving behind plus lots of space for posters and so on. Get the shop to supply the stand if at all possible, or go to a market trader's supplier.

Salespeople can be hired by the hour as needed. Consult a staff bureau. (Look under **Employment Agencies** in the Yellow Pages.) Try and get salespeople to suit the product. Attractive young ladies are suitable for many items, but one company sold masses of its special jams and preserves by employing two energetic grannies!

The operation of this sort of business is far simpler than the organisation. The skills used are very much like those of the market trader. You need plenty of noise and action to create a crowd. Then, demonstrate! Invite audience participation where possible. Invite tasting if appropriate. Bring out all the product advantages, use humour — even highlight the faults.

Experts on this type of selling say that few sales are made during the actual demonstration. Most people are too reserved. Instead, most cash changes hands immediately afterwards as people disperse, think, and then return to buy. Have lots of stock — and helpers — on hand to sell.

### How much can I earn?
Sales figures for this sort of operation are far higher than ordinary shop lines. In fact, one US trader (where this form of selling is more advanced) actually claimed takings of $11,450 in one day! A UK company selling a small cleaning item in department stores suggests daily net profits of £250 for a once-a-week, one-person demonstration stand. This should be considered low and could be much more for an innovative product.

### Summary
1. Choose the right products.
2. Select suitable positions in good stores.
3. Set up selling effectively.
4. Cut your losses, capitalise on your successes.

## PROJECT 10: A SHOP WITHIN A SHOP

| | |
|---|---|
| *Status* | Full-time, could be a sideline |
| *Capital required* | Moderate to high |
| *Return* | Longer term |

### In brief

A demonstration stand is a good way of testing a retail product or method. But it is not much more difficult to do the same on a permanent basis, that is, by opening a small shop unit within a larger shop, supermarket or department store.

This is now a popular concept in retailing and many large shops will consider renting off 500 or 1,000 square feet for a complementary (not competing) business. For example, department stores can feature toys, books, shoes or electrical items as a shop within the shop.

This sort of venture needs a good product idea. It could be something quite ordinary copied from a shop within a shop in another town. Or a product tested on a demo stand. The arrangement will need capital for stock, shopfitting and advance rent, though this could be less than half that of establishing an independent shop, perhaps £2,000 upwards.

In short, the costs of establishing and running a shop within a shop are a fraction of a normal retail shop, but the takings and profits need not be any less!

Start by contacting large stores locally who may have space to rent. They, and the terms of their own lease, will often determine the product you can sell. Surprisingly, many progressive shops may also help with professional retail guidance as to what you can sell within their shop and how to set up your project.

Further details on how to proceed will be found in **Project 9.**

## PROJECT 11: A SEASONAL SHOP

| | |
|---|---|
| *Status* | Part-time, occasional/seasonal |
| *Capital required* | High |
| *Return* | Very high, short-term |
| *Can be combined with* | Projects 9, 10, 14 and 20 |

### Project facts

Most shops trade on a continuous basis. This means balancing the profitable times (like Christmas) with the times of the year that only make a loss. It doesn't have to be this way though — a few shops operate on a seasonal basis, trading only in the good times, and dissolving for the rest of the year.

This gives rise to a lucrative one-off opportunity: the operation of a shop dealing in a specific line at the most profitable time of the year. Such a shop might make a fortune selling a job lot of stock, then closing and cutting losses when sales start to dive.

## What do I need?
● Capital for 1 month's shop rent in advance (say £200 upwards).
● Source of stock.
● Temporary sales assistants — recruit through Job Centres.
● Trade journals for the lines you want to sell, eg *Toy Trader* or *Shoe and Leather News,* will help identify suitable lines.

## Pros and cons

| Pros | Cons |
|---|---|
| Good for 'cashing in' on boom products | Not a continuous business with a regular income |
| Can be started with far lower overheads than a full-time shop | Stocks must be chosen carefully, avoiding products which are available cheaply because they have failed elsewhere |

## How do I operate?
First, you should plan in advance. Choose seasons and products that offer enormous scope at that time. Christmas is the boom time for many goods, like gifts and toys. Clothes or fashion accessories are good in the spring. Home furnishings and decorations sell well in the autumn. Discount household goods are appropriate to the New Year sale period.

Find a supply of suitable products at the time you want them. Use normal trade wholesalers, but look for special job lot bargains, e.g. discontinued stock you can get at knock down prices. Negotiate two months' credit from suppliers, so that you can sell many goods before you pay for them.

Next, rent a suitable shop. Seasonal shops must always be in busy town centre locations, as they don't have time to build up a reputation. Go to a commercial estate agent for help. It is often possible to find a shop that is between tenants at a low rent. Offer a month's rent in advance and no more. The maximum period of operation is usually three months.

Fit the shop out simply, using second-hand fittings from a shopfitter. Engage temporary assistants on fixed length temporary contracts. If you lack retail experience one of your assistants should be an experienced manager.

Open the shop when ready and operate as an ordinary sales outlet. The accent should generally be on the 'cheap and cheerful' side. Remember, there's no time to build a reputation so you can afford to cut service and quality in return for giving excellent value for money. This should produce enormous sales!

Sales from a seasonal shop may not be as high as similar, established traders take for the year. But the whole idea is that you close when takings start to dip (e.g. for a Christmas shop close a couple of days before Christmas) so you don't have to subsidise depressed trading periods from your profits. This is the concept behind the seasonal shop, and a formula that assures a quick, high profit.

## How much can I earn?

**Example:** A Christmas seasonal shop opened on 1 October selling toys, gifts, gift wrapping and cards. It closed on 23 December.

Takings for this period amounted to £55,000. The cost of a 'job lot' of stock bought in was £28,500, payable on 1 December. Three months' rent amounted to £2,400. Staffing costs were £2,750. Incidental expenses were £3,000. With all this taken into account the gross profit for this period was approximately £20,000.

**Example:** A shop selling similar lines traded all year round. Annual takings were about £120,000. Stock cost £56,000 and staffing costs were £13,000. 12 months' rent was £10,400. Incidental expenses amounted to approximately £5,000. The gross profit for this period was £35,600.

The full-time shop was open four times longer, but profits were only 50% more than the seasonal shop's. This difference is all due to trading only at the best time of the year — the unique seasonal shop concept!

## Summary
1. Choose your products carefully, and avoid those which are cheap because they have failed elsewhere.
2. You will need a good, busy site, because you do not have time to build up a reputation.
3. Fit your shop out with second-hand fittings to cut costs.
4. Cut back on quality and service so as to be able to offer knock-down prices.

# PROJECT 12: CLEARANCE SALE

| | |
|---|---|
| *Status* | Mostly part-time, occasional |
| *Capital required* | Moderate (can be high) |
| *Return* | Very high, fast |

## In brief

As a retail method the seasonal shop has many advantages, but it does require a larger amount of capital and gives a medium-term pay-back. For a smaller capital requirement and a short-term profit a clearance sale is a good alternative.

A clearance sale has many similarities to the seasonal shop. You look for and buy a source of bargain stock. The main difference is, however, that a hall of some kind is rented for one day to sell the stock. The event is publicised locally and all the stock cleared in one day to achieve maximum takings.

Buy stock as for a seasonal shop. Then co-ordinate delivery with the renting of a town hall or community centre in a busy location. Publicise the event locally with door-to-door leaflets and press advertising. Stack all the goods (linens, clothes and shoes are ideal) on tables, employing trustworthy part-timers to take the cash.

The aim should be to sell all the stock — and usually at bargain prices, too. The combination of low prices and the sale atmosphere can result in enormous daily takings, typically £3,000 or more for a clothes sale.

Although this activity is ideal for a 'one-off' business many entrepreneurs run it as a regular concern. Venues and products that pay off best can be repeated, and virtually anything can be sold as long as the price is low enough! Telephone possible local suppliers — manufacturers, distributors, wholesalers, market trader suppliers and import agents etc — to see if they have anything they wish to clear. Use the 'Yellow Pages' as an initial source.

Further details on how to proceed will be found in **Project 11.**

## PROJECT 13: MOBILE VIDEO LIBRARY

| | |
|---|---|
| *Status* | Mostly part-time |
| *Capital required* | High |
| *Return* | Good, long-term |
| *Can be combined with* | Project 23 |

### Project facts

Videotape rental has become very popular recently. However, there is a new trend emerging. On the one hand slightly declining demand means there is less support for video rental shops, while on the other hand in outlying areas there is a demand, but insufficient to justify opening a shop.

These problems have been solved by the introduction of the mobile video library, a development which makes this lucrative activity economic in terms of start-up capital and takings.

### What do I need?

- A supply of videotapes — consult a distributor for outright purchase or lease terms. You may find suitable contacts listed under **Video Libraries** in the Yellow Pages.
- Transport. A light van is best, you could use a motor-caravan. Consult local motor dealers or vehicle leasing companies (look under **Van and Lorry Leasing** in the Yellow Pages).
- Cash for advertising (suggest £300 upwards).

### Pros and cons

| Pros | Cons |
|---|---|
| Decline in demand for tape rentals through shops can be an advantage for this activity | Large start-up capital needed There is the risk of theft |

### How do I operate?

This business operates best in towns and rural areas where demand is insufficient to support a video shop and where distances to the nearest shops can be prohibitive for customers. It is not ideally suited to cities. Divide your area into 'rounds'. In the busiest areas you might visit every other day, other areas only weekly. Advertise your service widely. Leaflets and door-to-door calling are probably best. Explain your service thoroughly. It may take some time to become known.

Make a small membership charge, enrolling members on proof of address and a deposit against tapes rented (usually £10 or so). Issue a membership card.

At the agreed intervals tour the rounds with your van, stopping off at set points. This presents an opportunity for members to hand in old tapes and rent new ones. Tapes are charged for until the next time the van visits the area. This can be more than a shop would charge (perhaps double) but it is more convenient for the member.

The business is infinitely expandable — you can continue adding new rounds until it becomes a full-time activity.

## Summary
1. You will need a van or motor-caravan, and a source of videotapes — either to buy outright or to lease.
2. Divide your area into 'rounds', and advertise your service widely, through leaflets and door-to-door calls.
3. Enrol customers as members — charge a membership fee.
4. Charge a deposit on tapes borrowed — perhaps £10 — to give some protection against theft.
5. Charge rental on tapes according to the timing of your next round.

## PROJECT 14: GIFT WRAPPING

| | |
|---|---|
| *Status* | Part-time, occasional/seasonal |
| *Capital required* | Moderate |
| *Return* | Very high for time needed |
| *Can be combined with* | Projects 9 and 11. |

### Project facts
Some business opportunities are seasonal, but nevertheless, make more money in a short season than others do all year round. This is particularly true of Christmas business, and one example is a gift wrapping service. This could operate all year round in a small way, but be very busy indeed from October to December.

### What do I need?
- A site. The ideal place is a large shopping centre, but a large department store would suit. Many managers of such property do let space. Negotiations and bookings need to be started in summer for the following Christmas.

- An attractive stand, perhaps with about six or eight serving positions. Contract a shopfitter or market stall supplier.
- Gift wrapping supplies — paper, ribbon, bows and tags. Buy in bulk from a wholesale stationer. Use good quality ones, as the service attracts big-spending customers.
- Gift-wrapping assistants. Employ people part time to man the stand and wrap gifts. Housewives and students are ideal for pre-Christmas business.

## Pros and Cons

| Pros | Cons |
| --- | --- |
| Can be started with low overheads | Not a source of regular income |
| You could get 'subcontract' work from local shops, giving an almost guaranteed income | It might be difficult getting assistants who are sufficiently skilled |

## How do I operate?

Plan shifts so that the stand can be fully manned during shop opening hours. Ensure that you have sufficient supplies to suit peak demand.

The idea of the business is simple. Customers buying from nearby shops present the gifts they have bought. Your staff wrap expertly on the spot, collect the charge and then move to the next customer!

Very few shops offer this service, yet it is a great time- and money-saver for busy shoppers, as well as providing expertly and unusually wrapped gifts. Charges can range from £1 to £5 per gift for a good service. Wrap 4,000 gifts pre-Christmas for an excellent part-time return.

Some operators even do 'subcontract' work for local shops. That is, shops give vouchers for free gift wrapping at your stand — then pay you afterwards. So it can be much bigger business than a seasonal activity usually suggests.

## How much can I earn?

Existing gift wrapping services have reported takings of anything between £2,500 and £6,000 in a busy pre-Christmas period, with clear profits approaching 50% a possibility.

In the USA, where this is long established, some of the highly organised services report takings of $25,000. All this is from one pitch in a large and busy shopping centre. This doesn't necessarily mean a similar situation can occur in this country, but it does illustrate the scope!

**Summary**
1. Find a good site in a busy shopping centre.
2. Erect an attractive stand.
3. See whether local shops will 'subcontract' work out to you.
4. Recruit suitably skilled wrappers.
5. Charge between £1 and £5.

---

## PROJECT 15: GIFT DELIVERY

| | |
|---|---|
| *Status* | Part-time only |
| *Capital required* | Very low |
| *Return* | Moderate |
| *Can be combined with* | Project 93 |

---

**Project facts**
This is a novel service to develop. You can offer to deliver an attractive gift personally to the door of the recipient. Such a service is ideal for a special surprise, or a last-minute gift, and the prices charged are generally considerably higher than the value of the article given!

**What do I need?**
- Cash for advertising.
- Transport.
- Suitable products — you don't need to hold stocks, just buy as you need them.
- Attractive gift wrapping.
- A smart uniform for delivery staff is a good idea, but optional.

**Pros and cons**

| Pros | Cons |
|---|---|
| Very low investment | Needs heavy promotion |
| No stock risk | Only possible as a sideline |

**How do I operate?**
To start, choose products suitable for a gift delivery service. Bottles of spirits, wines and champagne, chocolates, flowers, tobacco and the like are all suitable. You need no stocks, simply buy from local shops or wholesalers as needed. In case of products

needing a licence to sell (e.g. alcohol) arrange things so that the customer buys the gift and you merely deliver it.

Advertise widely. Press advertisements are one option, but it is better to advertise in the shops where gift products are sold, such as off licences and florists. You could 'appoint' some shops as your suppliers. Provide them with attractive posters and leaflets promoting the facility.

Customers requiring the service should telephone their orders to you. If possible take credit card payments (consult credit card companies). Alternatively they could call into your appointed shops. A suitable product is selected, gift wrapped and delivered.

Such services are always ornate and well presented. Attractive wrapping is a must, together with speedy, courteous delivery, perhaps including a 'singing telegram' on delivery to the recipient's doorstep! The more professional the service the more you can charge — frequently many times the cost of the gift, and £7 or £8 at least.

## Summary

1. Advertise your service widely, through the press, but also by means of posters in shops supplying gift items.
2. You can buy stock from your suppliers as you receive orders, or your customers can order from the shop, with you providing the wrapping and delivery.
3. Accept credit card payments.
4. You will need attractive wrapping and a speedy, courteous delivery service.

## PROJECT 16: SIGN SUPPLY

| | |
|---|---|
| *Status* | Part-time, full-time |
| *Capital required* | Low |
| *Return* | Good, long-term |
| *Can be combined with* | Projects 46, 89 and 94 |

## Project facts

One business which has changed dramatically and quickly recently is the sign supply industry. Where once only hand-painted signs existed, there are now many alternatives for those wanting signs.

All this presents an interesting business opportunity in the supply of sign products. Simply promote a business offering 'a sign for all reasons', then supply customers through a network of different manufacturers and suppliers. You would never need to make or handle the products yourself with this system.

## What do I need?

- Reliable suppliers. Contact sign makers through the Yellow Pages. Introduce yourself as a sign supplier and offer to sell their products on commission. One good tip is to approach manufacturers and suppliers in regions of the country other than your own. The majority would be interested in expanding into new markets
- Magazines like *Exchange & Mart* and *Industrial Exchange & Mart* will contain possible contacts.

## Pros and cons

| Pros | Cons |
|---|---|
| Virtually no stock is needed | Skills in selling are essential |
| There is little competition for such a service | |

## How do I operate?

Good sign products are in great demand, from all types of businesses. Nowadays, a business sign can be an important form of advertising. One survey, for example, put the value of a good, small shop sign at £4,000 a year in advertising-value terms.

The best way to sell is to visit businesses in person (or employ a representative). Take literature from your suppliers to assist you. Discuss how signs can promote the business in question and suggest your products.

On securing an order from a customer take a 50% deposit and have the sign made up by your supplier, having first confirmed the price with them. When the sign is delivered, fit it at the customer's premises. (Use local builder or joiner if you need to). Collect the balance due on completion. Pay your supplier at the end of the month following delivery (normal trade terms) for a smooth cash flow.

Contact past customers from time to time as, if they are satisfied, they are likely to need further signs in future. This repeat business is one of the major features of this type of business and must be exploited to the full.

## Summary

1. Find a number of reliable suppliers, especially from outside your area.

2. Suggest to them that you sell their products on a commission basis.
3. Visit businesses in your area, selling your suppliers' products.
4. Take a deposit of 50%.
5. Order the sign from the supplier, and erect it for your customer, using a local joiner if necessary.

---

## PROJECT 17: ADVANCED DRIVING TUITION

| | |
|---|---|
| *Status* | Part-time, later full-time |
| *Capital required* | Very low |
| *Return* | Good |
| *Can be combined with* | Projects 1 and 95 |

---

### Project facts

Educational courses are always popular, and often the more practical they are the more successful too. One subject this could ideally apply to is driving.

Driving tuition is readily available for learner drivers. But one lucrative opening is in advanced driving tuition for more experienced road users. Evidence suggests that with ever busier roads this could be a service more and more in demand.

### What do I need?

- Tutors. If you are not sufficiently skilled advertise your requirements in the local press. Suitable people may be approved 'learner' driving instructors, or just experienced drivers, ideally members of the Institute of Advanced Motorists.
- By law learner driving instructors who charge for lessons must be Department of Transport approved. If your tutors are not they must only teach drivers holding a full driving licence in an advisory capacity.
- The AA and RAC publish a lot of useful information on motoring matters. Their addresses are: The Automobile Association, Fanum House, Basingstoke, Hants. The Royal Automobile Club, RAC House, Croydon, Surrey.

### Pros and cons

**Pros**
'Education' and the teaching of skills is a growth area

**Cons**
New idea, so may take time to get established

Long-term success will
depend on a good reputation

## How do I operate?

Advertise in the local press. Take the tack that you can help existing drivers improve their driving — make it safer, more enjoyable and more economical. Explain that it will reduce the risk of an accident, perhaps save them money on motor insurance and reduce wear and tear on their car. Sell the service on these benefits, not just on the fact that it is a course. You can also sell through companies or clubs and societies, perhaps offering a small discount.

Sell your lessons in courses, perhaps a minimum of four at a time. Up to £20 an hour could be charged for a good tutor. Pay the tutor one-third of this sum.

On receiving bookings make arrangements between the customer and the tutor for the lessons. The customers should use their own cars, suitably insured, to minimise the problem of providing cars.

Each tutor can decide the course content, but they should be asked to follow their own prospectus so that the pupil learns something practical and useful. Subjects might include car control; overtaking; night driving; dealing with skids; driving a performance, diesel or automatic car.

Such subjects are rarely covered in depth by existing instructors who teach to driving test standards. Hence, there should be sufficient concerned drivers who would appreciate being tutored in safe, useful driving techniques. This is just the sort of service that could be taken for granted in years to come!

## Summary

1.  If you do not have the expertise yourself, recruit experienced drivers as tutors - either existing 'learner' driving instructors, or members of the Institute of Advanced Motorists.
2.  Advertise your service, selling it on the benefits — safer, more economical driving.
3.  Charge for a course of perhaps four lessons at a time.
4.  Wherever possible, use the customer's car, suitably insured.
5.  The tutor can define the course content, but ensure that something useful is learned.

## PROJECT 18: OTHER DRIVING TECHNIQUES

*Status*      Part-time or sideline initially
*Capital required*      Low
*Return*      Moderate

### In brief

There is no reason why tuition should be restricted to car driving alone. It could just as easily be expanded to the driving and control of other forms of transport. As there are fewer alternative sources of tuition these could possibly be more profitable still. Examples of courses to offer are:

- Trailer/caravan towing. This is very useful, but very rarely offered elsewhere.
- Motorcycles. Courses for the motorcyclists do exist, but there is great potential for increase, with backing from concerned adults.
- Commercial vehicles. Even quite large commercial vehicles can be driven on a car licence, yet the driving techniques involved are completely different.

In each case thoroughly research the regulations that apply to each form of transport to see if they constrain your operations. The Highway Code is your first point of reference. Always employ suitably experienced and/or qualified drivers to operate your courses.

Start with some local research. Check out the demand and availability of trained instructors. A small newspaper advertisement could be placed and response monitored before major arrangements are made.

Further details on how to proceed will be found in **Project 17**.

## PROJECT 19: TOUR GUIDE

*Status*      Part-time, occasional
*Capital required*      Low
*Return*      Good, short-term
*Can be combined with*      Project 94

### Project facts

Tourism is a huge and growing industry and there are many

lucrative ways to service it. One valuable but little-known service is acting as a tour guide in resorts and areas popular with tourists. It is a service that can be a lot of fun, and extremely satisfying, as well as financially rewarding.

Operating as a guide is the ideal owner-operator activity, but it is also suitable for operation as a 'desk' business with a small number of hand-picked employees. Proximity to an area with tourist interest is vital, but few other resources will be needed.

## What do I need?
- Proximity to a tourist area – vital for this kind of venture!
- A suitable stand in a prominent position.
- Possibly a licence from your local authority.
- An interest in your subject and a pleasing manner.

## Pros and cons

| Pros | Cons |
|---|---|
| Low investment | Requires a lot of walking |
| Can be satisfying as well as rewarding | Only occasional/seasonal |

## How do I operate?
Select an area of operation, and specialise in it. This can be coast, country, town or city, but should attract good numbers of tourists. For this reason, business may be seasonal.

Check with the local authority to see if a guide's licence or membership of a society is required. They might also limit the fees you can charge.

Research your area at the local library and/or museum for detailed, interesting information. With maps and notebooks, devise a tour route taking in points of interest on the way. If necessary, employ part-time guides, who should be keen and knowledgeable, and brief them on the route.

Set up a stand with attractive signboards in a prominent position. If possible, arrange to use a shop as a meeting point for the tour. (It will generate business for them, too!)

Advertise in the local press, tourist guides, tourist offices and with travel agents, hotels and taxi drivers. You could get some of this advertising free — or you may have to pay a small commission.

Organise tours to depart every half, one or two hours, according to demand. Customers assemble, pay their fee and are taken on the conducted walking tour of the area in question. Continue along these lines to suit demand. You could operate three guides from 10am to 8pm in peak season. You could expand to cover different routes, which will get you repeat business, start tours by taxi, coach, pony and trap and bicycle. You could branch out into 'theme' tours, such as 'wildlife in the city' or a pub tour!

## How much can I earn?

The typical fee for a 1 – 1½ hour walking tour of, for example, a historic city might be between £3 and £5. Each tour could take up to twenty customers with a minimum usually of eight. At busy times such tours could operate half-hourly in suitable areas.

Of this fee income the guide would typically keep 20-25%. The rest goes to the organiser as profit, though about 30% of the cost of each tour should ideally be ploughed back into advertising to build up custom.

## Summary

1. Select an area to operate which gets a lot of tourists.
2. Research thoroughly the area you intend to cover.
3. Set up a stand in a prominent position.
4. Advertise through the local press, tourist guides, travel agents, hotels and taxi drivers.

---

## PROJECT 20: FLOWER SELLING

| | |
|---|---|
| *Status* | Mostly part-time |
| *Capital required* | Low |
| *Return* | Small |
| *Can be combined with* | Projects 14, 21 and 23 |

---

## Project facts

Most businesses face a choice of premises, usually between working at home, or from an office, shop or workshop. But there are a few businesses which do not require premises, and can thus save you a fortune in start-up costs and overheads.

One such opportunity is street trading — simply selling anything on the streets. Low costs don't make street trading an instant business, but what you sell can dictate how successful you will be.

Flower selling was at one time a popular street trading activity. Now it is becoming popular again as one of the many booming 'novelty' businesses. It offers an economical owner-operated business, or a chance to start a larger concern than finances would otherwise allow.

## What do I need?

- Possibly a licence.
- Suitable flower sellers.
- Large wicker baskets for displaying flowers.
- The trade journals *The Grocer* and *Nurseryman and Garden Centre* might provide useful information and contacts.

## Pros and cons

| Pros | Cons |
|------|------|
| Low investment | Fairly small return |
| Flower selling is becoming popular again | May be difficult to keep a check on sellers |

## How do I operate?

First, you need to investigate local street trading laws and get a licence if you need one. Then engage flower sellers. Part-time girls are ideal and smart uniforms and large wicker baskets for displaying the flowers will enhance the presentation and customer appeal.

Decide on pitches. Choose busy undercover locations. You might perhaps agree with a shop owner to trade in their shop doorway for a small set rental.

Arrange a supply of flowers from the nearest wholesaler. (Look under **Flower Wholesalers** in the Yellow Pages.) If necessary, take advice from a florist on suitable types and presentation. Then each day, you should collect the flowers and deliver them to flower sellers at their pitches. At end of the day you collect the proceeds.

Flower selling is one of those quaint trades from the past and, like many things, would be welcomed back to many a town and city. In many ways you are selling an attractive service, rather than the actual product — make buying a pleasure. In fact you could substitute a wide range of other products. Flowers are just the most convenient. Products that capture the imagination and are attractive are better for street trading than any functional product or service.

## Summary

1. Investigate the need for a licence.
2. Engage part-time flower sellers if you are not going to do the selling yourself.
3. Decide on the best pitches.
4. Buy fresh flowers from a wholesaler each day, and deliver them to your sellers.

5. At the end of the day, do the rounds of your sellers, collecting the proceeds.

---

## PROJECT 21: SELLING FADS

| | |
|---|---|
| *Status* | Part-time, occasional |
| *Capital required* | Moderate to high |
| *Return* | Very high, fast |
| *Can be combined with* | Projects 23, 25 and 33 |

---

### Project facts
Consumer products are subject to many trends and fads. Products that are hits one month are often completely unwanted the next. This sort of problem plagues the regular retailer. However, it can be a big advantage to the entrepreneur looking for an occasional, high-profit, sideline business.

### What do I need?
- A site – usually a street stall or a stall within a shop.
- Stock of an item which could become a fad.
- A flair for identifying a fad.
- Trade journals concerned with consumer goods, eg *British Clothing Manufacturer* or *Gifts International* might provide ideas on new products.
- *Sell's Directory of Products and Services* may provide leads, as long as you act quickly when it is first published each July. Published by Sell's, 39 East Street, Epsom, Surrey.

### Pros and cons

| Pros | Cons |
|---|---|
| Profit margins can be very high | A lot of research is needed to identify fads |
| If you get it right, you can sell enormous amounts in a short time | If you get it wrong you can be left with a lot of unsaleable stock |

### How do I operate?
The fad dealer needs to keep a close eye on the market for consumer goods. Read trade publications, import journals, and develop contacts with progressive wholesale warehouses. Keeping an ear to the ground is a vital part of the business. The commercial section of a main library is the place to track these contacts down,

using the many different trade directories.

The fad dealer should look for innovative products that will catch the public eye. These should be things that have enormous novelty value and sell on sight — anything that's a bit unusual and special.

There have been all kinds of fads over the years. Ball point pens were once fads and 'magic' puzzle cubes are one of the best examples. Digital watches sold for less than a £1 are another. The whole idea of a fad is that it sells in huge numbers when it first becomes known — enough to make enormous profits. Someone made millions selling 'pet rocks' in California. Yet, once the boom period is over it might disappear completely, or settle down to a much slower sales volume.

When you think you have discovered a fad buy in some stock. There is a good deal of trial and error in this. But fads can usually be bought cheaply with sky-high profit margins, thus reducing the risk.

The next step is to devise a sales method. A popular method is a street stall or stall within a shop. Or you could sell at a fete, country fair, Sunday market, or race meeting. For more promising-looking items a shop could be rented on a short lease. Employ temporary staff to handle all the sales work.

The aim of selling a fad is to move as much of it as possible over a short period. The best products can sell thousands of pounds' worth from a street stall over a couple of days — all quick, hard cash profit. Once sales start to decline the trader usually discontinues the product, leaving others to take the smaller rewards. He moves on to new and more lucrative fads!

The trade in fads is rarely full-time. But just a few well-chosen products over the course of a year can generate several times the takings from any more ordinary form of trading.

## How much can I earn?
**Example:** Consider the case of the enterprising trader who one year decided to open up a small kiosk selling souvenir items for a well-known pop star. These were obtained from a wholesaler who had imported them from the USA and consisted of posters, badges, T-shirts, mugs etc.

A sea front kiosk was rented in a major seaside resort from May to September. It was rented from the local council for £2,250. The 'job lot' of stock cost £3,400 approximately. Staff to man the kiosk cost £2,500 (£2 per hour), and other costs (rates, electricity etc) were £830. All these costs were paid in instalments, so only £500 was needed 'up front'.

Sales from the kiosk for the trading period totalled £16,500 (about £750 per week). Costs totalled £8,980, so approximate profits from the project were £7,500 over a summer alone.

## Summary

1. Keep a close eye on developments in consumer goods. Read the trade publications and develop contacts with wholesalers.
2. Look for innovative and novelty products.
3. Buy stock, set up your stall or shop, and employ temporary staff.
4. When sales start to decline, stop selling that item.

## PROJECT 22: SPECIAL INTEREST WEEKENDS

| | |
|---|---|
| *Status* | Mostly part-time, possibly full-time |
| *Capital required* | Low |
| *Return* | Very high, short-term |
| *Can be combined with* | Project 1 |

### Project facts

There are almost endless money-making opportunities in the leisure industry. Some of them are ideal for exploitation on a quick-return basis, one prime example being in organising special holiday break weekends

One idea you may have heard of is the 'murder' weekend, an established venture where a crime is restaged at a hotel — and the guests play detective! There are many simpler versions, however, that offer great scope for a business project

### What do I need?

- Organisational ability.
- Ideas for hobbies or leisure interests that could be covered.
- The *Good Hotel Guide,* available at most libraries, is a good source of venues.
- *Hospitality* is the trade journal for the hotel trade and might have some leads.
- The British Hotels, Restaurants and Caterers Association, 40 Duke Street, London W1M 6HR, might be of assistance.

## Pros and cons

| **Pros** | **Cons** |
|---|---|
| Leisure and hobbies are a growth industry | Losses possible if weekend fails to sell<br>Some 'trial and error' may be needed to establish most successful weekends |

## How do I operate?

Decide on a theme for your weekend. It should preferably follow a hobby or interest, e.g. a train-spotting weekend, a theatre weekend, a fishing weekend and so on. Contact a suitable hotel and arrange to hold the venture there, perhaps in a conference suite. They may well not charge for the facilities because of the extra room, restaurant and bar custom you bring.

Organise a programme for the weekend, perhaps a dinner-dance on the Friday evening, a Saturday morning film, a demonstration on the Saturday afternoon, a quiet dinner that evening, and Sunday free for leisure. Bring in guest speakers and demonstrators if necessary.

Advertise the weekend thoroughly in regional and national newspapers and magazines read by the enthusiasts you are trying to attract. The hotel may also have its own publicity officer who can help. Take bookings, with deposits, in advance. On the actual weekend you can either attend to organise the course, and ensure all goes well, or leave it in the hands of the hotel, perhaps for a small extra fee.

You can expand this idea by duplicating successful events in other regions, and by holding different weekends in your original hotel.

## How much can I earn?

Profit margins can be adapted very much to what you expect to earn.

**Example:** One 'natural history' weekend at a 3-star hotel sells at £99 per person and usually attracts 80 guests. This provides takings of £7,920. The hotel charges £45 each for 2 nights' accommodation and meals. This leaves a net income of £4,320 less administrative expenses and costs of speakers and events (about £800) to be paid for.

## Summary

1.  Decide on a theme — preferably a fairly popular hobby or interest.
2.  Contact a suitable hotel and make arrangements to hold your venture there.
3.  Organise a programme around your theme, bringing in expert speakers or demonstrators where necessary.
4.  Advertise the weekend thoroughly in the magazines read by your target audience.
5.  Take bookings in advance, with a deposit.
6.  You can attend the weekend yourself to ensure there are no hitches, or leave it to the hotel.

---

# PROJECT 23: A VAN SALES ROUND

| | |
|---|---|
| *Status* | Part-time/full-time |
| *Capital required* | Moderate |
| *Return* | Good, especially long-term |
| *Can be combined with* | Project 98 |

---

## Project facts

Most retail methods need a shop, or at least a shop position of some kind. However, there are some which don't and which can therefore save an enormous amount in start-up costs and overheads. One such method is a van sales round.

The sales round method of selling to shops in particular has developed enormous popularity, and many shops now buy some of their stock this way. It's an ingenious way of combining salesman and delivery driver in one, making a service that is efficient, cost-effective and which attains high sales figures.

## What do I need?

*   A source of stock.
*   Large capacity transport — try a local commercial vehicle dealer.
*   Drivers and sales staff combined.
*   A small sales office (can be at home).
*   The sales trade journal *Selling Today* could provide useful techniques. It is available at major libraries.
*   Customer contacts can be found through the *Stores, Shops and Hypermarkets Directory,* available at main libraries but probably worth buying for this business from the publishers (48

Poland Street, London W1). Also make contacts for selling, and buying stocks, through the Yellow Pages.

## Pros and cons

| Pros | Cons |
|------|------|
| Van sales save on start-up costs | It may be difficult to find a cheap source of supply |
| Lower costs mean more resources devoted to selling | |
| It is a popular way for shopkeepers to buy | |

## How do I operate?

Choose stock to sell. This can be anything that shops buy to resell. Products like bread are established and probably too competitive. Sweets on the other hand are popular lines. One advantage is that it doesn't matter if you start with a product that fails — it costs little to try something else.

A supplier will need to be found, ideally a manufacturer or an importer. Wholesalers, apart from very large ones, are generally not suitable as prices will not be low enough. Cash is needed to buy in at least a van-full of stock to start.

You can start with one van and driver, but two or three would be better for a larger business. Lease vans through motor dealers who can also arrange to fit out the interiors for your stock. Advertise for combined drivers/salesmen. They should be experienced, and you should pay a basic wage plus sales commission.

If the salesman is experienced he will know how to operate, but it is helpful to plan a strategy, identifying shops which are likely customers. The great thing is, though, that you can visit dozens of customers in a day and make sales there and then.

The whole idea of the van sales round is convenience for the shopkeeper. He can see and get the stock he needs instantly. Similarly, you can benefit from lucrative impulse sales. You can also encourage a shopkeeper to try stock he would not otherwise sell which could become a regular line.

To help sales, stock is supplied on credit, then invoiced on monthly terms from the sales office daily. The job of the office is also to ensure that the van is fully stocked at all times.

Selling anything can never be completely simple, but one advantage of a van sales round is that costs are so much lower and you divert more resources into the actual selling than into administration. Profits can be directed straight into expanding the rounds.

## Summary
1.   Decide what you are going to sell.
2.   Find a supplier — usually a manufacturer or importer.
3.   Lease your van or vans.
4.   Hire drivers/salesmen on a salary-plus-commission basis.
5.   Supply customers on 30 days' credit.

## PROJECT 24: A PRESS AGENCY

| | |
|---|---|
| *Status* | Full-time |
| *Capital required* | Moderate to high |
| *Return* | Good, long-term |
| *Can be combined with* | Project 46 |

## Project facts
News is a highly saleable commodity and there are many ways of selling it. A straightforward way is simply to collect local news, process it, and then sell it on to newspapers. This type of service is generally known as a press agency. It is suitable for a low-capital start-up business which could develop into a considerable concern.

## What do I need?
●   A small office (can be at home) with a typewriter and a telephone. A wordprocessor, facsimile machine and use of telex will help.
●   Transport.
●   At least two television sets and two or three radio sets, plus a regular order for all local and regional newspapers.
●   Part-time help, ideally someone with journalistic experience.
●   Trade publications such as *Benn's Media Directory, Willing's Press Guide* and the *Writers' and Artists' Yearbook,* available at main libraries but probably worth buying for this business, are a good source of buyers.
●   The trade journal is the *Journalist* (available from main libraries).
●   The *Yearbook of World Affairs* and *Whitaker's Almanack* will provide information for many story leads.
●   The National Union of Journalists, 314 Gray's Inn Rd, London WC1X 8DP, and the Institute of Journalists, Bedford

Chambers, Covent Garden, London WC2E 8HA, are the professional associations.

- *How to Write Articles That Sell* by Perry Wilbur, published by Wiley, could provide useful tips.

## Pros and cons

| Pros | Cons |
|---|---|
| Once established, income can be considerable and regular | Can take time to establish — income can be small to start with |
| Can become a national and international business | Attention is needed 24 hours a day, 7 days a week |

## How do I operate?

The idea of a press agency is the efficient gathering of 'raw' information from your region and its distribution to 'out of area' publications, who will pay for news they can incorporate into their pages.

Properly organised this need not be difficult. The idea is to monitor all local news services for interesting stories. Choose mainly things that are of national interest — from court news to sport to human interest and humorous stories. Read the local papers daily and monitor TV and radio news all day.

When an interesting story appears through these media send a reporter to the scene to gather first-hand information. Then write it into a concise press report — between 200 and 1,000 words. Do not directly copy another report. Make what you write suitable for splitting down into smaller news lines for incorporation in other newspapers.

Before gathering the news find buyers for it. These are ideally regional and national newspapers and some magazines, from outside your area. Possibly other press agencies would be interested in buying your news too. Track them down through a press directory.

Telephone or write to possible buyers identifying yourself as an agency. Most will at least consider new news sources. They will either offer to take all your news output, or just that on selected subjects. They will probably pay a set fee, and this can be negotiated.

Develop as many customers as possible as they can all be supplied with the same information. Then the procedure is to gather stories daily, write them up, and distribute them to buyers. This needs to be done as quickly as possible via telex or facsimile machine or even telephone.

Customers will pay monthly for the stories they use, even if they take just a couple of sentences from your original report. They will also tend to take more as your reputation increases. After all, buying news in this way in much cheaper for them than employing reporters direct. This is the whole idea of the press agency. You might try specialising — sports news, business news, foreign news, showbiz news, and so on.

You can expand on an infinite basis, covering more news, more areas and finding more customers, perhaps becoming a major regional or even national supplier of news!

## Summary

1. Find buyers for your service among newspapers and magazines from outside your area.
2. Monitor all local news, from newspapers, radio and television.
3. You may need to employ a reporter to cover some stories.
4. Gather stories daily, send your own reporter to get the on-the-spot story if necessary, write them up, and distribute them as quickly as possible to your customers.

# PROJECT FILE 2
## Office and Desk Businesses

The projects in this chapter can all be run from an office or desk, or over the telephone, often without leaving home. They will therefore appeal to people whose commitments may prevent them from working away from home. Many could also be operated as evening or weekend ventures.

## PROJECT 25: OPPORTUNITIES IN INTERNATIONAL TRADE

*Status*               Part-time, later full-time
*Capital required*     Moderate
*Return*               Very High
*Can be combined with* Projects 21, 61, 90 and 95

### Project facts
These days trade is more international than national as countries specialise in products which other countries seek out. Importing and exporting are established activities and much of this business is handled by agents.

The agent's job is to find a supply of goods in one country, then a demand in another, or vice versa. At the moment British goods can readily be exported to the EEC, while consumer goods are big imports from the Far East.

### What do I need?
A telephone (and maybe access to a telex through a bureau) is vital.

- Quality business notepaper and a typewriter.
- A talent for negotiation is useful.
- A city branch of a bank to provide help with import-export generally, as well as international finance.
- SITPRO (Simplification of International Trade Procedures Body) have a kit explaining import-export procedures. Price £10, from SITPRO, London SW1Y 6BR (Tel.01-214 3399).
- British Overseas Trade Board (BOTB) provides Government help for exporters. 1 Victoria Street, London SW1H 0ET (Tel.01-215 7877).
- HM Customs & Excise will advise on licences, regulations, restrictions and duties. Mark Lane, London EC3 (Tel.01-283 8911).
- A number of groups and societies bring importers and exporters together, for example the London Chamber of Commerce and Industry, 69 Cannon Street, London EC4N 5AB (Tel.01-248 4444) and the Institute of Export, World Trade Centre, London E1 9AA (Tel.01-488 4766).
- The Government Export Credits Guarantee Dept (ECGD) helps protect against the risks of exporting and not getting paid. It runs an insurance scheme, thus facilitating more

extensive exporting than would otherwise be possible. Details from ECGD, Aldermanbury House, Aldermanbury, London EC2P 2EL (Tel.01-606 6699).

- A useful, if rather technical, book on the technical and documentary aspects of international trade is *Elements of Export Practice* by Alan E. Branch, published by Chapman and Hall (1979).
- Most major trading countries have directories of products and services available (and sometimes firms looking to buy). Check at main libraries. In the case of the USA, for example, Thomas's registers are directories to look for. This is in addition to international telephone and telex directories.
- Several international periodicals advertise for UK importers and exporters.
- Wade World Trade, Wade House, Swindon, SN1 1RJ (Tel. (0793) 613161), publish *Sales & Marketing Management,* and also have a correspondence course in international trade.

**Pros and cons**

| Pros | Cons |
|---|---|
| Profits can be very high for a moderate investment | Requires a lot of initial research |
| | There may be complex legal requirements |

**How do I operate?**

Most agents operate by finding a product in the UK then a buyer overseas, or an overseas product and a UK buyer. You can however start with a demand and find a product to suit it.

Because of the help available from BOTB, exporting can be a good starter. Look in the Yellow Pages or *Manufacturers & Merchants Directory* (available at libraries) for UK manufacturers of interesting export items. Offer to become an agent and sell their goods overseas. Then offer the products to overseas wholesalers or importers by advertising in foreign newspapers or writing to them direct. Details of overseas traders can be found in foreign telephone and telex directories at major libraries. Start with a good product — for example, quality UK goods export well to the EEC, the Middle East and the USA and Canada.

To import, write to the London embassies of suitable countries. (Find them in *Whitaker's Almanack)* Their trade delegations will put you in touch with associations or manufacturers and exporters who may have goods for export to the UK. Again, start with a good product — consumer goods from Korea, Thailand, Taiwan, Japan and China usually sell well.

The best way to operate is to prepare neatly written and printed details of the products you have for sale giving full specifications. Then send these to the potential buyers you have tracked down from earlier research. Subsequently negotiate deals personally with buyers and sellers. Keep your negotiations in writing (or by telex).

Be prepared to send out large quantities of enquiries in order to match a supply with a demand. Allow for the cost of this in your start-up capital. Use a translation bureau for foreign language material (cost £20 to £40 per thousand words).

When a deal is struck you should leave the original seller to complete the deal, deliver it and collect payment. Few agents ever actually handle the goods directly. An optional delivery service can be offered through a freight forwarder. Contact one through the Institute of Freight Forwarders, 9 Paradise Road, Richmond, Surrey TW9 1SA (Tel. 01-948 3141).

**How much can I earn?**
Agents are paid by negotiable commission — 10% would be typical. Within this, orders can run to thousands or even millions of pounds. One agent reported an annual contract worth £2 million on good commission terms, while still working part time from home!

**Summary**
1. Only act as broker/agent. Never buy goods yourself, to limit the risk.
2. It is important to project a really smart professional image.
3. Trade in proven products and with accepted countries to start.
4. Do your initial research thoroughly.
5. Leave the deal once it has been agreed. Let others handle the arrangements.
6. Follow up past contacts for lucrative repeat deals.

# PROJECT 26: PROPERTY RENOVATIONS

| | |
|---|---|
| *Status* | Part-time/full-time |
| *Capital required* | High |
| *Return* | Very high |
| *Can be combined with* | Projects 36 and 81 |

## Project facts

As new house building slows from previous peaks the demand for renovated property is greater than ever. There are numerous opportunities for taking dilapidated old property and transforming it into modern new accommodation.

Previously this opportunity was only open to property tycoons, experienced builders and the like. Now beginners can successfully buy and renovate old property and sell at a considerable gain. Although the capital required may be high, if you proceed on a syndicate basis individual amounts will be much lower.

## What do I need?

- Management skills.
- The ability to present proposals and arguments convincingly.
- The capital to buy the first house, or a syndicate of people prepared to invest.
- Good professional contacts — see under **How do I operate?**.
- The periodical *The Estates Gazette,* 151 Wardour Street, London W1V 4BN, contains useful information.
- *Doing Up a House* by Mary Gilliat, published by Bodley Head, the *Readers Digest DIY Manual,* published by Readers Digest and *Property Renovation Profits,* published by Chartsearch, 14 Willow Street, London EC2A 4QJ, are books on the subject.

## Pros and cons

| Pros | Cons |
|---|---|
| Very high return | Needs considerable |
| Property seldom loses | managerial skills |
| value | Planning and building |
| | regulations could present |
| | problems |

## How do I operate?

This is a compact business that can be run from home. Large amounts of capital are not essential, as you can trade as a syndicate. You invite others to form a limited company or partnership with you. They inject capital and you supply the organisational skills. Each person takes equal shares in the company and equal shares in the profits.

First you need to assemble your team of professional advisers. Your role is that of manager and organiser, and you should employ experts to do the actual work. The experts you need are:

— Estate agents. Contact a number, and tell them you are interested in buying property suitable for renovation.
— A bank. Banks can provide help with financial planning, and also with mortgages and overdrafts to finance the project. Alternatively, you might try a building society.
— A solicitor. He is vital, both when it comes to buying the property and to advise you on the law as it relates to development. It is best to find one by personal recommendation if possible.
— A surveyor. He can help by surveying the property and advising you on whether it can be renovated economically. He can also do some design and supervisory work. Contact the Royal Institution of Chartered Surveyors, 12 Great George Street, London SW1P 3AD (Tel. 01-222 7000), for the names of local ones.
— An architect. He will attend to the details of your renovation once a property has been selected. Contact the Royal Institute of British Architects, 66 Portland Place, London W1N 4AD (Tel. 01-580 5533), for the names of local ones, and ask for a quote on fees first.
— An accountant. He will help to arrange financing, prepare accounts, deal with tax and apportion profits between syndicate members. It is best to find one locally by personal recommendation if possible.
— A builder. He will do the actual renovation, under the direction of the architect or surveyor. Obtain quotes from at least three builders. The professional associations are the Federation of Master Builders, 33 John Street, London WC1N 2BB (Tel. 01-242 7585) and the Building Employers' Confederation, 82 New Cavendish Street, London W1M 8AD (Tel. 01-580 5588).

Having assembled your team of professionals, you are ready to start. A typical project may run as follows:

1. Advertise in the 'Business Opportunities' or 'Finance Required' columns of newspapers. This will find people with capital who wish to join together as a property development syn-

dicate. Then form a legal syndicate of investors with each as a partner.

2. Look for properties via estate agents. Deal only in residential property. Make a shortlist.
3. Instruct your surveyor to examine each for renovation potential.
4. If the surveyor approves instruct the architect and builder to design and cost a renovation, and the solicitor to check the legal position.
5. If the accountant indicates that the project is viable, instruct the solicitor to buy the property.
6. Finalise the plans with the surveyor and builder. Get planning consents (your surveyor will help here).
7. Prepare a schedule of works. The surveyor and architect will arrange and supervise the work.
8. When completed, put the property up for sale.
9. The accountant divides the proceeds equally between the syndicate members.

## How much can I earn?

Assume five investors provided £15,000 each to buy a £40,000 barn and convert it for a further £35,000. The barn might sell for £150,000 in which case each member would get £30,000 back, representing 100% return on their original capital of £15,000.

Most renovators work on the same basis, finding and renovating property after property. The process of 'gearing' means a larger project can be undertaken each time, allowing profits to mount up. One example is a renovator who started with £20,000 from mortgaging his home. Two years later he had built up a portfolio worth £2 million!

## Summary

1. Deal only in residential property. Small terraced houses and cottages are ideal. (Commercial property is much riskier.)
2. Form a syndicate of investors. This is better than borrowing money and there is rarely a shortage of willing investors, whose money can be secured on the property.
3. Retain professional advisers.
4. Work only in a supervisory capacity. A manager's time is far too valuable to become involved in building work.
5. Always resell renovated property and reinvest quickly.

## PROJECT 27: PROPERTY DECORATION

| | |
|---|---|
| *Status* | Part-time, possibly full-time |
| *Capital required* | Low |
| *Return* | Possibly very high, short-term |

### In brief

Full-scale renovation offers good financial rewards, but you don't always have to undertake such major works to gain them. Frequently, property values can be increased substantially by clever redecoration alone.

Sometimes, property hangs on an estate agent's books just because of dilapidated decorations, or possibly an unusual or old-fashioned colour scheme. Underneath the property is basically sound and a good 'economy' redecorating job adds value.

A typical way that decorating adds value is by painting an entire interior with white paint, then laying plain carpet throughout; or putting an untidy garden entirely under a lawn.

To operate this venture, look for houses that have been on the market several months and are in poor decorative order. Buy them as for renovation, taking the advice of a surveyor on 'before' and 'after' values. Redecorate to a tight budget, then offer for sale at a new higher price.

Experienced decorator/renovators report excellent margins on this sort of operation. In one recent example such a project easily added 10% to the value of a house costing £60,000 — ie £6,000, of which the cost of the work was a small fraction.

Further details on how to proceed will be found in **Project 26.**

## PROJECT 28: FINANCE BROKER'S AGENT

| | |
|---|---|
| *Status* | Mostly part-time |
| *Capital required* | Low |
| *Return* | Very high |
| *Can be combined with* | Project 3 |

### Project facts

Finance is big business and, quite apart from corporate finance, there is plenty to be done at the smaller end of the scale, with small personal loans and mortgages. There are numerous finance brokers nationwide with money to lend. Many of these require agents to find customers for them. As an agent you merely advertise for and sign up clients for loans, in return for a commission. The lender supplies and collects the money.

Any business dealing with personal finances requires a high degree of integrity and confidentiality, together with a good standard of general education . The project would probably best suit those who, in addition, have a sound financial track record in business and who can capitalise on their experience and contacts.

### What do I need?
- A small amount of capital (£100 or so) for advertising.
- A telephone.
- Transport.
- The ability to deal with people confidentially.
- Financial institutions requiring agents advertise in the *Exchange & Mart, Daltons Weekly, Daily Mail, Mail on Sunday* and *Sunday Express* amongst others.
- The professional organisation is the Corporation of Insurance and Financial Advisers, 6 Leapale Road, Guildford, Surrey GU1 4KX (Tel. (0483) 39121).

### Pros and cons

| Pros | Cons |
| --- | --- |
| High return for low investment | Needs a good selling manner |
| You simply act as a middle-man, with no financial risk | You may have to have a licence |

### How do I operate?
To act as agent a Consumer Credit licence is normally required. This is usually readily granted as long as you abide by the Office of Fair Trading Codes of Conduct. For details apply to the Office of Fair Trading, Field House, Bream's Buildings, London EC4A 1PR (Tel. 01-242 2858).

Next, contact sources of finance and enquire about registering as their agent. If your background is suitable you might be able to persuade them to employ you as an agent in your area. This might restrict you at first if your desire is to be self-employed but you would have the protection of trading as part of an established company while you acquired experience and it may obviate the need for you to have a licence of your own.

Banks do not work this way, but a number of finance houses do. They advertise for agents in Sunday newspapers. Send for 'agent kits' from a number and compare terms.

Most finance houses will offer various types of finance, secured loans and mortgages being the most popular. Each pays you a commission for each client obtained. This is typically 10% for a secured loan, but it does vary so do check.

Familiarise yourself with the details of the financial packages, Then advertise your services. The most common method is local newspapers. Also consider leaflets or shop window cards. Rules on advertising financial services are strict. The OFT have a booklet, or refer to the Advertising Standards Authority, 2 – 16 Torrington Place, London WC1E 7HN, for a copy of their guidelines.

Enquiries are usually taken by phone. Subsequently the agent either visits the home of the enquirer or sends an application form (supplied by the lender). A few initial questions can filter out unsuitable applicants and help the agent decide the best type of loan package for the successful ones.

On completion of the application the agent decides which of the finance houses he deals with can best supply the facilities, taking into account the terms offered both to the client and himself. The application is then forwarded direct to them.

Finance houses take over the entire process from there on. They check the status of the applicant, process the loan and pay the balance, as well as administering repayments. At no time is the agent's money involved. Finance houses usually pay their agents commission at the end of the month. With this operation there is no restriction on the income that you can accumulate. The amount you earn will depend on the work you put in.

It is best not to conduct any investment business or give any investment advice under this project as by law this may require membership of a professional association such as FIMBRA. See the next project for further details.

## Summary

1. Apply for a licence first.
2. Register with several finance houses, so that you can offer a wide range of facilities and competitive terms.
3. Don't underestimate the amount of advertising required to build up business. Advertise in all local papers every week.
4. Canvass past customers for repeat business whenever possible.
5. Ensure you are well informed so that you can give the best possible service.

## PROJECT 29: OTHER FINANCIAL SERVICES

*Status*  Part-time/full-time
*Capital required*  Low
*Return*  High

### In brief

There are also opportunities to establish agencies in other financial services. These generally operate in exactly the same way as finance broking. It is preferable though, to operate only in one field at the start of business. Later, the facilities of one agency can be offered to customers of the other.

Other opportunities include:

- Insurance plans
- Pension schemes
- Investment schemes
- Personal equity plans, unit trusts etc

In most cases companies in these fields require agents to find clients on commission. They advertise in the same places as those requiring finance brokers.

Proceed as in **Project 28**. However, the law requires agents for most investment services to be members of a recognised professional body, such as the Financial Intermediaries, Managers and Brokers Regulatory Association (FIMBRA), Tel. 01-929 2722.

If you are unable to qualify as a member of a body, and some newcomers may not, then it may still be possible to trade by working as the appointed representative of one of the established firms offering investment propositions who are members. Consult existing investment companies to see if they make such arrangements. If they do ask a solicitor to advise you what your legal position is.

If necessary, the skills needed in this project can be gained more easily by operating as a finance broker not handling investments. See the previous project.

# PROJECT 30: MARKET RESEARCH

| | |
|---|---|
| *Status* | Mostly part-time |
| *Capital required* | Very low |
| *Return* | Good, short-term |
| *Can be combined with* | Projects 2, 16, 32 and 46 |

## Project facts

Market research is a service large companies find invaluable. It quite simply tells them what their customers want. Small businesses, however, are rarely offered this facility and have to leave this important matter to chance.

There is definitely an opening to offer an efficient service researching markets and demand for small businesses. Very few businesses are not ready to spend money in order to make money!

## What do I need?

- Office space at home, or a small office in a professional area.
- A telephone, a typewriter, good business stationery.
- The ability to converse with small business owners.
- Part-time helpers to conduct interviews and surveys.
- The professional body is the Association of Market Research Organisations (see telephone directory for local contacts). They have a code of conduct which will help you provide a good and ethical service. Also there is the Market Research Society, 175 Oxford Street, London W1R 1TA, who also publish the *Market Research Handbook*.
- A further useful guide is the *Handbook of Market Research* by Robert Ferber, published by McGraw-Hill.
- For best results, study the needs of your customers through their own trade journals. For example, if market researching for grocers *The Grocer* is the publication to read.

## Pros and cons

| Pros | Cons |
|---|---|
| It is a service many small businesses need but are not getting | Questionnaires need careful preparation |
| Easy to set up | |
| Service generates considerable customer interest | |

# How do I operate?

Your service will offer market research to small businesses, telling them what customers want, and thus giving the information they need to improve trade. Most small businesses don't have time to do this themselves. As a result they can waste time by trying to sell products no one wants, or they might lose money by neglecting to sell things people want to buy. Your service is very much geared to increasing efficiency and directly increasing profits.

To start, research the customer potential for the service. Most types of small business are potential customers. Shops are ideal, but small tradesmen, professional practices, garages and home-based businesses are also good. You might do market research for the local grocer, or the local estate agent!

Contact firms by personal call, telephone or a well-written letter. On average 10% of those solicited might be interested enough to call you. Arrange a personal appointment with each so you get a good opportunity to explain your service.

At the personal visit it is important to explain that by knowing customers' views a business can try to meet customers' needs better. Rehearse a 'sales pitch' if necessary. Suggest how just a 5% increase in turnover as a result of your survey could make a significant difference to the annual profits. If the enquirer is interested quote them a price for a market survey of their business. This could range between £300 and £1,000.

You must then devise a survey which will provide the information they require. One possibility is a postal questionnaire of customers, but a better method is by using research interviewers to ask questions. Employ housewives part-time for this job.

First, devise a suitable survey, perhaps of 5 – 10 questions. The exact nature will depend on the type of business, but generally, you will be asking for customers' opinions on the service, the products sold, the staff, the appearance of premises and so on. Draw up the questions carefully, then type them up and photocopy them, allowing one copy for each expected interviewee.

Next, send your researchers out to conduct the necessary interviews. You might decide that they should visit past customers of the company, or (especially for shops) they might ask questions in the street outside the shop, or door-to-door in the vicinity. Stress impartiality and courtesy at all times.

For a typical survey you might collect 200 customers' opinions. The data is then returned to you for analysis.

The next stage is to analyse results, so that you can give the customer useful information from the scramble of customers' answers. The best way to do this is by means of a written report, perhaps 2,000 – 3,000 words long. What you write depends on the business, but try to make it a factual summary of the questions and comments made and be careful not to change any meanings.

In the case of a grocer you might say how often the average shopper shopped there, what they bought mostly, what they bought elsewhere — and why they didn't buy it here. All these points would be of invaluable help to any grocer. When the report is complete it should be neatly typed and bound. Take a copy to the customer. Indeed, as well as giving them the report you can discuss it in detail. This will help them glean the maximum possible information.

An important and profitable part of the service is to repeat the operation, say six months later. In this way the owner will be able to judge the value of your service, perhaps by seeing how the improvements made as a result of your survey have improved trade.

### How much can I earn?
**Example:** One actual small home market research company reports healthy demand from businesses in the under £500,000 turnover bracket. They have recently carried out a probing survey for a small independent supermarket for £550 (two days' work). A free house pub was charged £300 for an evening 'exit poll' of drinkers to assess their product preferences. They also hope to gain a commission for £3,500 of survey work for a local motor trade franchise.

### Summary
1. Organise yourself professionally. If you give a competent impression customers will assume you are experienced, even if you are new to the business.
2. Visit potential customers in person to sell your service.
3. Write the questionnaires yourself, but get impartial interviewers to do the asking.
4. Produce a factual written report of your findings and discuss it with the customer in person.
5. Aim to get repeat commissions. This is a business where satisfied customers will recommend you to their colleagues.

# PROJECT 31: TELEPHONE MARKET RESEARCH

*Status*                         Mostly part-time
*Capital required*               Low
*Return*                         High, short-term

## In brief

There is a way of starting a market research business on an even lower budget. Yet it is conceivably even more lucrative than **Project 30**. This is market research by telephone.

The telephone is an ideal market research tool. You can reach thousands of consumers at relatively low cost. The main requirements are two or three telephone lines and researchers experienced and confident in the use of the telephone.

This business operates in exactly the same way as 'on street' research, but can serve larger manufacturing and service businesses as well as shops and small businesses. Visit a customer, devise your survey, then select people to be interviewed through the telephone directory.

This service can also be used for the preparation of national opinion reports, for example, on political matters. A survey can be undertaken and then the results sold to press, TV and radio for news purposes. These outlets will commission surveys from well-established research organisations.

The disadvantage of this service is that research is biased towards telephone subscribers. However, the costs of running the service are lower, while charges tend to be significantly higher than conventional market research.

Proceed as for regular market research but see what demand exists before you commit yourself to a business launch. This business can be inexpensively tested by canvassing potential customers by telephone.

# PROJECT 32: ADVERTISING CARDS

| | |
|---|---|
| *Status* | Full-time/part-time |
| *Capital required* | Low to moderate |
| *Return* | Very high short-term |
| *Can be combined with* | Projects 2, 45 and 46 |

## Project facts

For most businesses, good advertising is a basic requirement but it is not always easy or cheap to procure. As a result, there are plenty of opportunities for the enterprising person to *create* sound advertising alternatives to present to hard-pressed businesses.

One interesting new advertising idea is the 'ad card', where a card describing participating businesses is circulated door-to-door. This gives much of the effectiveness of newspaper advertising with the cost-effectiveness of leaflet distribution.

The advertising card presents a business opportunity in itself. The potential can be tested with little capital, all you need is a phone! It is suited to 'one-off' operation where a continuous business is not required.

## What do I need?

- A good designer.
- Distributors.
- The journal *British Printer,* available in main libraries, might provide useful information.
- The trade bodies are the Advertising Association, Abford House, 15 Wilton Road, London SW1V 1NJ and the Institute of Practitioners in Advertising, 44 Belgrave Square, London SW1X 8QS.

## Pros and cons

**Pros**

Once established, income is regular and considerable

Capital requirement is low for a business of this type

**Cons**

Competition may exist in some areas

## How do I operate?

Quite simply, you seek advertisers to take a small space on a well-designed and printed card, charging a fixed fee. The card is distributed to homes locally. The nature of the card makes it a handy reference point for householders who are inclined to retain the card rather than throw it away as with other advertising. Hence, for a reasonable fixed amount, local businesses can enjoy continuous advertising at a fraction of the cost of the only real competitor — the Yellow Pages.

You can get customers with almost no outlay. A few telephone calls, from home, are sufficient to illustrate the potential.

The best way of selling is to telephone or visit potential customers in person. These include all local businesses who sell their products or services locally. Any business from a local garage to a plumber is suitable. Explain the concept of the ad card carefully. No sales literature is needed, but be sure to present a professional image, perhaps leaving a high-quality business card after the visit.

Businesses which are interested agree to take a space on the card for a fee. You distribute the card to a number of homes. A typical fee for a 1in x 2in space might be £200. This compares well with press or directory advertising in terms of value for money.

When the card is full it is published as an attractive leaflet. It is best to use a coloured A5 card, printed on both sides, then encapsulated in a plastic wallet. About twenty businesses can be covered. It is also a good idea to put some important local telephone numbers on the card (doctor, council offices etc) to add to the user value, and improve the chances of its being kept.

Have the card designed by professional designers, then typeset, printed and covered by a large firm of commercial printers. It must be of the very best quality so that, in most cases, it will be retained and used by the householder. Cards usually cover an area of 2,000 — 5,000 homes. Print accordingly.

The next job is to distribute the cards to homes. You can do this directly by employing door-to-door distributors, but the easiest way is to use a local distribution firm. These are frequently the same firms who distribute the area's free newspapers.

Check after distribution where possible. The better the card is received and used the better the response it will generate for the advertiser. If the advertisers are satisfied then they will more seriously consider repeating their order for subsequent cards.

**How much can I earn?**
This business makes an excellent one-off business, but it also offers ample scope for expansion. You can repeat the card annually in each area; publish cards in several areas (8 – 10) in your region; publish a larger card and charge more; or distribute to more homes

and charge more.

**Example:** If you sell 20 spaces on an ad card at £250 each, your income is £5,000. To design and print 5,000 cards would cost about £650, and to distribute 5,000 cards using a distributor would cost about £75. Your net income (before your own expenses, phone calls, transport etc) is therefore £4,275.

---

## PROJECT 33: DEALING IN SURPLUS STOCK

| | |
|---|---|
| *Status* | Part-time/full-time |
| *Capital required* | Very low |
| *Return* | High, fast. |
| *Can be combined with* | Projects 25 and 39 |

---

### Project facts
Millions of pounds of shop stock go to waste annually, not because it is faulty, but because it is in the wrong place at the wrong time. Quite simply, the product that sells out in one area may sit on the shelves for months in another!

This problem has given rise to a lucrative new service — the stock broker. He is a shrewd entrepreneur who matches a supply of surplus stock with a demand, and makes an attractive commission on the deal. The opportunity is home based, requiring a telephone and good negotiating ability. No cash or storage space is required as stock can be sold directly between shops.

### What do I need?
- A telephone.
- An ability to negotiate.
- Good business stationery.
- *Manufacturers and Merchants Directory, Sell's Directory of Products and Services* and *UK Kompass Register of British Industry and Commerce* will be useful in building up a list of customers.

### Pros and cons

| Pros | Cons |
|---|---|
| Offers fast, high rewards | Needs good negotiating ability |
| Can be operated without the need to see the stock | Significant risk of losing money in the event of a mistake |

## How do I operate?

You must set up professionally. Good business stationery and business cards are essential. Offer a '24-hour hotline' for sellers. Advertise your service widely, using retailers' trade magazines and local press. (Look in media directories at main libraries to find them.) Telephone or call personally on local traders or write to them, offering to sell their unwanted stock for cash.

With stock 'on your books' you should aim to sell it quickly. Telephone or write to other traders nationwide who may be interested. (Look for contacts in the Yellow Pages.) One idea is to publish a weekly bulletin of what is available and mail it to other shops.

When you receive an enquiry for stock negotiate between both parties. Usually, sellers sell at rock-bottom prices to clear stock they can't sell, while buyers may settle for wholesale price less only 10% – 20%. Arrange transport to the buyer via a haulage firm. The buyer usually pays, but sometimes it is the seller.

Supervise the exchange of payments and claim your commission, which could be £50 or £2,000 depending on stock involved.

To expand, you could offer a service to manufacturers, wholesalers, importers or large store groups, operating in exactly the same way but for larger amounts of money.

## How much can I earn?

**Example:** Shop A has 20 TV sets it cannot sell as nearby competitors are selling a more modern model. They place them with a stock broker, who circulates details and finds an interested shop (B). They sell in a small town with no local competition, hence they can control the local market. Shop A sells 20 sets for a total of £5,000 at a loss. The broker sells to Shop B for £6,000, making £1,000 commission. Shop B sells at £399, making about £40 more per set than if they had bought them from their wholesaler in the first place.

## Summary

1. A good professional image is essential.
2. Advertise widely.
3. Aim to sell any stock you acquire quickly.
4. Arrange transport when you have sold the stock and negotiated between the buyer and the seller.

## PROJECT 34: CREDIT CONTROL

| | |
|---|---|
| *Status* | Part-time/full-time |
| *Capital required* | Low to moderate |
| *Return* | Good, long-term |
| *Con be combined with* | Projects 28 and 87 |

### Project facts

Business cash flow is all-important and means the difference between a profit and a loss. Yet few small businesses have time to chase accounts — they need an effective service to gather that all-important money owed.

Such services exist already, but they are mainly expensive factoring services for larger companies. A small, economical service has a large untapped market of small business people to serve.

### What do I need?

- A small office with a telephone (could work at home).
- A typewriter and photocopier — you could computerise the system.
- A good telephone manner.
- Basic accounting, book-keeping and administration skills.
- Possibly a licence from the Office of Fair Trading, though this is sometimes unnecessary if the business is structured in a certain way. Details vary with prevailing legislation so check the current situation first. The Office of Fair Trading is at Field House, Bream's Buildings, London, EC4A 1PR (Tel. 01-242 2858). Usually, a licence will be readily granted to those of good standing, as long as trading practices continue to be reputable. The Consumer Credit Act is the appropriate legislation.
- The main banks publish useful information on credit and financial control. Ask for details and study similar schemes which you will find advertised in the Yellow Pages under **Credit Investigation Services.**

### Pros and cons

| Pros | Cons |
|---|---|
| Can be operated cheaply from home | Needs book-keeping and administrative skills |
| A much-needed service for | Needs care so as not |

small businesses                           to upset your customer's
                                           customers

## How do I operate?

This is an opportunity where you can get customers before
organising the actual service. The best method is to prepare a
short sales letter (like the one on page 100) explaining the service.
Then circulate it to small or medium-sized businesses in your
region. Virtually any business which offers credit is a potential
customer.

Visit interested parties personally to discuss details. The main
thrust of your sales pitch should be that you will handle all their
credit control, getting payments several weeks before they could
themselves. Charge a small percentage of each invoice collected
(2½% – 5%) or a flat fee per week for each account handled.

The operation of this business is based on accurate work.
The aim is to supervise the issue of company invoices and ensure
that they are paid according to the agreed terms, thus producing
a better cash flow for the customer. You will need to persist with
those who owe money, but getting invoices paid perhaps a month
or two sooner is not prohibitively difficult. Just keeping close tabs
on an account can speed up the payment routine.

When your customer issues an invoice to their customer they
should send a copy to you. Place this copy in a file indexed by
payment due date.

When the payment date comes up send a reminder letter to
the debtor. This may well elicit payment. If it does your customer
notifies you of this and you cancel the procedure.

If no payment results either send a printed standard reminder
letter to the debtor at two-, four- and six-weekly intervals after the
due date. These should be simple and clear and request payment
by return. Alternatively, telephone them to discuss the matter.
This usually gets a better response.

If the account is unpaid after eight weeks contact your customer
direct. They should contact their customer and make a personal
appeal for payment or, alternatively, instruct their solicitor to
initiate court recovery action after about twelve weeks.

At all times payments are made to the customer. You handle
no cash. Handling of the collection should be by post or phone,
remembering that undue harassment of debtors is illegal.

## How much can I earn?

Large firms have proved the undoubted value of this service,
so it is something that smaller companies can benefit from. In

**EXPRESS CREDIT CONTROL SERVICES**
2nd Floor, 166 City Road, Anytown. Tel. 234567

Dear Sirs

<u>How to Get Your Customers to Pay Sooner!</u>

If you sometimes have difficulty getting customers to pay your invoices we now have a new service which will get them to pay up faster, and relieve you of the tedium of monitoring and chasing tiresome overdue accounts!

Express Credit Control offers a professional supervision service for sums of money owed by your customers. Quite simply, from the moment you issue an invoice we follow it up to ensure it is paid, as far as possible within your credit terms, thus improving your cash flow, making available extra finance to run your business, and saving you time and staff costs.

Our service gets results, but it is courteous enough to avoid offending your valued customers. Many, in fact, will admire your efficiency in monitoring their accounts.

We really do feel we could be of assistance in smoothing the running of your business. And, if you would like us to explain how the service works, and how little it can cost, please telephone and ask our representative to call.

The money owed by your customers is valuable to your business. And, by getting it into your bank account sooner you stand to increase efficiency and boost profits. We can do that for you!

Yours faithfully

for EXPRESS CREDIT CONTROL

A sample sales letter offering a credit control service

one example, a company reckoned it could bank on an agency collecting 80% of accounts within fourteen days of becoming due. Previously, when credit control was part of their book-keeper's job few accounts were paid within 30 days from due date, and at least 35% were overdue by 60 days or more.

The income from this service is variable according to the amount of business you wish to handle. A typical small business client might issue invoices totalling £2,000 each week so, if you charged 2½% commission on invoice value, that would represent a weekly income of £50 from that customer. You could easily have seven or eight customers, for an income of £400 per week, and the business would still be part time. Larger businesses might handle twenty or thirty individual clients.

## Summary

1. Send a short sales letter to potential customers.
2. Charge a percentage of the value of each invoice collected or a flat fee per week.
3. File your customer's invoices by date, and when payment becomes due, send a reminder.
4. If no payment is forthcoming, send letters at regular intervals.
5. If no payment is forthcoming after eight weeks contact your customer. After twelve weeks, he should be instructing his solicitor to take legal action.
6. Payments should be made direct to your customer, not to you.

## PROJECT 35: HOUSE EXCHANGE

| | |
|---|---|
| *Status* | Mostly part-time |
| *Capital required* | Low |
| *Return* | Good, could be seasonal |
| *Could be combined with* | Projects 37 and 38 |

## Project facts

The linking together of householders who want to swap homes for holidays is a fairly new and innovative idea. It does, however, provide an excellent basis for a lucrative business, initially perhaps as a sideline but later full-time.

Assume you live in a small city flat. How nice it would be to have a holiday or short break in a country cottage! Yet there are country cottage owners who would enjoy city life for a while. The solution is simple — swap homes. You certainly won't get more homely or economic accommodation, which is the great appeal of this service.

## What do I need?
● A good accommodation address.
● Capital for advertising.
● *Willing's Press Guide* will help in locating newspapers and magazines to advertise in.
● Consult similar types of service or directory, such as *Summer Jobs in Britain* (published by Vacation Work International and available in main libraries) to see how they operate.

## Pros and cons

| Pros | Cons |
|---|---|
| Easy to operate | Could be seasonal |
| The clients make their own arrangements | May take time to get established |

## How do I operate?
Consult your solicitor on any legal aspects of this venture. Then set up a professional-looking operation. You can work from home, but if you do use a smart-sounding accommodation address. Look for properties advertised in local newspaper columns.

Advertise your Holiday Home Exchange Service in newspapers and popular magazines. It is probably best to start with those you know in your region. Prepare a professional colour brochure and application form to send out to enquirers. This should explain the concept of your service. The form asks for details of the applicant's property.

People wishing to exchange their home for a holiday residence must register with you. The charge for this would be at least £25, and could be as much as £50. This is still far cheaper than a hotel holiday!

At three-monthly intervals you publish a directory of homes for exchange, giving concise details and contact numbers. Mail the directory to all those registered. Sell copies of the directory (perhaps £3 a copy) by advertising in newspapers and magazines or perhaps through bookshops. (Contact a wholesale distributor to arrange this.)

Parties should contact each other to arrange the swap and all other details — you have no responsibility for leases, insurance etc that they might arrange between themselves.

Satisfied customers mean you can repeat this project annually, a further fee being charged each time. Over time you could expand the service world wide!

## How much can I earn?

Returns from such a service are best in the long term, but offer high annual profit. Consider that a new service might register 500 'swappers' and sell a further 5,000 copies of the directory annually. On top of this you could receive advertising revenue (from resorts or tourist attractions) in the directory. So the typical income from just one annual directory might be:

| | |
|---|---|
| Registration Fees: 500 x £30 | £15,000 |
| Directory Sales: 5,000 x £3 | £15,000 |
| Advertising Sales: Approx. | £4,500 |
| TOTAL Income | £34,500 |

Your printing and distribution costs would vary depending on the quality of the directory. But these might range between £1,000 and £3,000 for 5,000, plus administration and advertising expenses.

## Summary

1. You must have a professional-looking operation. If you are going to work from home, use a smart accommodation address.
2. Advertise your service and prepare a brochure to send to prospective clients.
3. Charge a fee for clients to register with you.
4. Prepare a directory of homes available for exchange, to be sent to everyone registered with you, and sold to the public.
5. Clients make their own arrangements for the actual exchange.

---

# PROJECT 36: SOUVENIR PLOTS OF LAND

| | |
|---|---|
| *Status* | Part-time, could be full-time |
| *Capital required* | High |
| *Return* | Very high, long-term |
| *Can be combined with* | Project 86 |

---

## Project facts

Land is a prestige possession, ownership of which confers some standing. This status has been used to effect in a novel little business enterprise — the sale of 'parcels' of land, complete with the ownership and usage rights. These parcels make a really unique novelty gift or possession.

This opportunity already operates in a few locations, but can be copied in others. For example, in the Scottish Highlands one entrepreneur offers ownership of a country estate from as little as £10, complete with title of 'Laird' (Scottish landowner)! This comprises a 1ft square plot in an attractive lochside estate, complete with right of access.

Although plots are of little practical use they make a great novelty product, and are ideal as a gift with a difference! They also offer a superb business opportunity, since the 'souvenir' value of the land is considerably greater than its value in any other context.

**What do I need?**
- Capital with which to buy land.
- A solicitor to clear legal aspects.
- The ability to sell the concept of souvenir plots.

**Pros and cons**

| Pros | Cons |
| --- | --- |
| An excellent 'novelty' product with enormous scope | Some capital outlay is needed |
| You sell land at a value far in excess of what it would have realised otherwise | The whole project depends on suitable land being available in a country or moorland area |
| | Legal advice is essential — this could be costly |

**How do I operate?**
Look for suitable plots of land. Areas of natural beauty are best as this gives a good 'conversation' sales angle. Contact land agents in suitable attractive areas (look under **Land Agents** in the Yellow Pages). Alternatively, advertise in *Farmer's Weekly*. Plots without planning permission for building can be extremely cheap. Check the legal aspects of what you propose to do with your solicitor. Usually you would buy land in the normal way and resell it in 1ft square plots by means of a simple licence-type deed, which you can issue without a solicitor and without expense.

Advertise in newspapers and magazines of all kinds. The classified columns in national newspapers are suitable. Make being the 'owner of a country estate' sound compelling! Prepare a smart but simple printed brochure for enquirers. You can get customers to send in £10 or £20 for a 1ft square plot and in return you send them their deed of ownership. Make it an attractive 'parchment scroll' type of document, suitable for framing.

You administer the land for the owners, selling more plots to pay for the upkeep. You might perhaps keep some yourself as an investment. Owners have the right to visit and use the land on which their plot is based as part of the 'novelty' value, though very few will, which makes maintenance and supervision very simple.

The whole idea of a souvenir plot holds immense novelty value and makes an exciting possession. It's also a great way of making land of very little value quite valuable.

## How much can I earn?
**Example:** A one-acre plot of land in a remote country area sold for just £2,000. Lack of planning consent meant it had no development or even agricultural use. Within that area there are 43,560 1ft square plots! The entrepreneur divided them on a scale map and offered each for sale at £15 each. The total value was £653,400! It may take several years to sell a large number (2,350 had been sold after 3 years) but even with a number of plots unsold this offers an excellent return.

## Summary
1.  Check the legal implications with a solicitor.
2.  Look for suitable land, preferably in a country area.
3.  Advertise in newspapers and magazines for buyers, and prepare a smart brochure.
4.  Charge £10 – £20 for a 1ft square plot.
5.  Send buyers an attractive 'parchment' type of document to register their ownership.
6.  You administer and maintain the land.

---

# PROJECT 37: A DATING AGENCY

| | |
|---|---|
| *Status* | Part-time/full-time |
| *Capital required* | Moderate |
| *Return* | High |
| *Can be combined with* | Project 41 |

---

## Project facts
Many businesses succeed by bringing supply and demand together. One that does this on a much more personal basis is the dating agency or introduction bureau. Good bureaux are in demand. It

is a business a thoughtful person can set up on an individual basis, probably from home.

## What do I need?

- Capital for administration systems and advertising.
- A considerate and confidential approach.
- Office address in a prestige area.
- Administrative ability.
- Preferably a personal computer with a database system, though this is not essential.
- *Willing's Press Guide* will help locate publications for advertising. The magazines *Computing* and *Computing Today* (available from major newsagents or libraries) may give some advice on computer applications, if you are using a computer. Also consult *Computer Users' Year Book*.

## Pros and cons

| Pros | Cons |
| --- | --- |
| Once operating, it can be very lucrative | Clients' applications need to be carefully analysed to avoid embarrassing mistakes |
| | Can take some time to become established |

## How do I operate?

The first step is to set up a system for introducing compatible people. The usual arrangement is for them to fill in a form which lists certain hobbies, pastimes, sports and likes or dislikes, such as eating out, travel, pop music. To each subject they give a score from 1 (dislike) to 10 (like). When a number of questions have been answered the scores are formed into a numbered code.

When several forms are gathered they can be compared. Codes nearest to each other indicate compatible people who could be introduced to each other. For a small business the comparisons can be done manually. For a larger one a personal computer can be used. Employ a specialist programmer to devise a programme.

Advertising is an important matter. An advertising agency could be employed for a larger concern, or you could try small ads in magazines and newspapers. A brochure is a must. Have it professionally produced and printed to explain and sell your service. Each brochure should include an application form.

Fees for such services can be considerable, but they should be linked to the quality of the service. £50 for providing introductions over a three-month period would be a minimum. For a top quality service £200 for a month might be quite reasonable.

When business first starts you may have to wait three months or so for sufficient members to register. Tell all your clients this. Thereafter though, the service is much simpler. As a new member registers you simply compare their details with others already registered and bring together compatible ones. This can be done by hand, but a microcomputer can cut the work involved. As you match each applicant with suitable contacts send them details of their names and addresses. They do the rest!

The results clients get in their introductions will owe a great deal to the care exercised in 'matching up'. So although there are many existing bureaux this is an opportunity for a new business to compete effectively with a personal service.

After gaining some experience a more comprehensive service can be offered by personally interviewing new members, or even video recording interviews for showing to potential 'partners'. Such a service generally has a far higher success rate for satisfactory matches, and the fees can therefore be considerably increased.

## Summary

1. Advertise widely, using an agency if your budget will run to it, or otherwise in personal columns.
2. Get clients to fill in a form listing their interests and likes or dislikes, to enable you to match their requirements.
3. Compare new clients' forms with those of people already on your register to find compatible 'partners'.
4. As the operation gets bigger, you will almost certainly need to use a computer.

---

## PROJECT 38: A CONTACT SERVICE

| | |
|---|---|
| *Status* | Part-time/full-time |
| *Capital required* | Moderate to high |
| *Return* | High, fast. |
| *Can be combined with* | Project 41 |

---

### Project facts

Contact or pen-pal services are reasonably popular, but a new idea takes this a step further. A new service from the USA runs a contact service for hobbyists and enthusiasts in all forms of sports and hobbies.

This is an opportunity that can be duplicated several times over. It needs no more than a talent for careful organisation and administration and is a typical desk business.

## What do I need?
- Organisational and administrative skills.
- *Benn's Media Directory* and *Willing's Press Guide* (available at main libraries) will provide ideas for places to advertise.

## Pros and cons

| Pros | Cons |
|---|---|
| Capital requirement is low | Fairly new idea, so |
| Enormous potential if the idea 'takes'. | could take time to establish |

## How do I operate?
The hobby contact service is easy to operate. The aim is to put people with similar hobbies and interests in touch with each other for discussion and friendship. Evidence suggests that such a service is popular, whether for plane-spotters, anglers or stamp collectors.

Advertise the service in hobby magazines serving several popular hobbies, such as fishing or photography. Then prepare a leaflet explaining the service to send out to enquirers with an application form.

Interested parties return the application form giving personal details like name, address and age and details of their hobby, together with a one-off fee of about £20. You wait until other like-minded people enrol, and match each form with similar forms to establish where their interests coincide. You can have a computer programme devised for this (consult a computer retailer or specialist).

Send each applicant the address of one compatible enthusiast. Each applicant also has their address sent to two or three other people. They are then left to get in touch with each other and correspond, converse, even meet, as they prefer.

If the applicant requires further contacts you could make these available at a 'privileged member's rate' which would be about two-thirds of the normal rate. Alternatively, if a user is dissatisfied because nothing genuinely comes of his contacts, you could release some further addresses on a complimentary basis.

This service can expand to whatever size you require. By nature, the vast majority of people like meeting and talking with others with similar interests. This sort of service is an excellent way of pursuing an enjoyable hobby or interest.

The service should be accepted well in this country, with a potential for 10,000 – 12,000 members if it is well promoted. The fee income could certainly be attractive at around £20 per member annually. One major advantage is that it can be tested for a very low outlay.

## Summary

1. Advertise your service in hobby magazines.
2. Send an explanatory leaflet and application form to enquirers.
3. When clients return their forms, match them up with like-minded enthusiasts.
4. Send each applicant the name and address of one other person, and leave them to make any further contact.

---

## PROJECT 39: COMPANY SALES AGENT

| | |
|---|---|
| *Status* | Part-time/full-time |
| *Capital required* | Moderate |
| *Return* | Very high, long-term |
| *Can be combined with* | Projects 3 and 4 |

---

### Project facts

With many estate agents now operating it's easy to sell a house. But it's far harder to sell a business. There are business transfer agents, but they tend to offer mostly 'newsagent and grocery' type businesses. If you have a limited company or a share in a business to sell, it's much harder to find a buyer.

This problem opens the opportunity to start up as a company sales agent. These agents work on a similar basis to house agents, but instead sell companies and interests in companies. They are strictly professional operations and ideal for those with executive experience.

### What do I need?

- A telephone.
- Quality business stationery.
- Executive experience is useful.
- A solicitor and accountant are essential.
- *Dalton's Weekly* is the premier publication for advertising businesses. It is a good place to advertise, but will also give you an insight into the existing trade in businesses.

## Pros and cons

| Pros | Cons |
|------|------|
| The individual commissions involved can be very large for a small outlay | Competition in some areas<br>Commissions are only paid once a sale goes through, so there could be cash flow problem |

## How do I operate?

First, contact and retain a solicitor and an accountant. Ask them about the legal side of selling businesses and get them to help with any future problems.

Advertise your service in quality newspapers and business magazines. Start with your major regional newspaper. Handle enquiries professionally and personally. Quote enquirers a price for selling their business. A typical fee might be 1% commission for businesses valued at up to £350,000, and ¾% for those worth £350,000 and over. If necessary ask a surveyor and accountant to help with valuations.

You can advertise businesses for sale in the classified columns of quality newspapers and business magazines, including *Dalton's Weekly*. Also prepare a monthly 'gazette' of businesses available and distribute it to accountants, solicitors, insurance brokers, investment and management consultants. They will all have clients looking to invest in sound businesses.

If the business you are selling is a private limited company, UK law prohibits the advertising of shares for sale. You will have to offer the business operation only, making it clear you are not selling the company as such.

When enquiries come in issue written outline details of the business, including extracts from the last three years' accounts. Place buyers that are seriously interested in touch with sellers. It's usual for their respective solicitors and accountants to handle the details. You can help with the negotiations, but leave it mainly to the professionals. Be prepared for some negotiations to fail, but when the sale goes through collect your commission.

Keep repeating the process. Some accountants and other professionals may become regular customers, buying businesses for their clients for investment purposes.

## How much can I earn?

The scope for this activity may seem to be limited but it is, in fact, quite considerable. Selling companies can be a haphazard business, but becomes viable with good organisation. The profits can be considerable as manufacturing and service companies generally have much higher values than the corner shop!

**Example:** One company sales agent has recently sold a small engineering company for £280,200 at 1¼% commission (£3,502) as well as a quarter share in a garden centre for £155,000. He currently has for sale a self-drive car hire firm for £90,000 plus stock at a value of £135,000, at 1% commission terms. He has received an enquiry from an investment company wishing to sell an independent supermarket chain for a price in the £1.9 million region. They are offering ½% sales commission (£9,500) plus payment of all advertising costs and a 'quick sale' bonus of up to £10,000.

## Summary
1. It is essential to retain a solicitor and an accountant.
2. Advertise your service in quality newspapers and business magazines.
3. Handle enquiries professionally and personally.
4. Advertise businesses for sale in quality newspapers and business magazines, and prepare a monthly 'gazette' of businesses available for distribution to accountants, solicitors and other professionals.
5. If the business you are selling is a private limited company, you are not allowed to advertise shares, only the business operation.
6. When enquiries come in, issue details of the business.
7. Negotiations will normally be handled by the buyer's and seller's solicitors and accountants.

## PROJECT 40: TELEPHONE SERVICES

| | |
|---|---|
| *Status* | Mostly part-time |
| *Capital required* | Very low |
| *Return* | Good, fast |
| *Can be combined with* | Projects 30, 42, 87 and 88 |

### Project facts
The telephone is an important business tool. It also offers opportunities to start lucrative services such as representation, advertising or selling. Such ventures are ideal for home start-up, but can also grow to considerable concerns. Some ideas for the latest in telephone services are given here.

**What do I need?**
- A telephone, perhaps several lines, and an answering machine.
- A pleasing telephone manner.
- The Office of Telecommunications (OFTEL) monitors and regulates telephone facilities, and can help with queries. They are at Atlantic House, Holborn Viaduct, London EC1N 2HQ (Tel. 01-353 4020).

**Pros and cons**

| Pros | Cons |
|---|---|
| Profits can be high, for little investment | There is some competition — your service must be very professional to compete |
| It is highly flexible — you can take on as much or as little as you like | The service may need to be offered 24 hours, 7 days a week |

**How do I operate?**
Before starting any service of this type contact British Telecom to discuss your plans. They can supply details of the latest equipment available. They will also advise on the present call rates so that you can calculate your business expenses.

The best customers for such a service are local small businesses. Sell to them by telephone or personal calling. There is a range of services you can offer.

You could, for example, act as a telephone agent. Offer your number for businesses to use as a 'branch'. This gives them local representation where customers may prefer approaching local firms. You simply take calls and pass the message on to them. For example, an insurance broker based in London would receive far more enquiries if he had agents in Cardiff, Manchester and Glasgow acting as 'branches', and using their telephone numbers in his advertising.

Another service could be a message service. Here you take messages for people who are unable to be near a telephone during the day. For example, a self-employed plumber may move from job to job during the day but need a regular telephone number to quote in his advertising.

Telephone selling is popular nowadays, and generally quite successful. Employ 'chatty' people to canvass potential customers for home services and the like. Find their numbers from the telephone directory. Such a service is quite acceptable if organised professionally!

Alternatively, companies undertaking widespread advertising campaigns may not have the necessary resources to handle a lot of telephone enquiries. You could offer to do this on a contract basis during the period of the promotion. For this you would need a 'bank' of telephone extensions, or perhaps answering machines. As potential customers telephone in response to the advertising you simply pass on their enquiry or arrange for the despatch of a brochure.

There are in fact a number of useful business services you can offer using a telephone. The advantage is that they can be as simple or as complex as you want them to be to suit your time and capital resources.

## Summary
1. Contact British Telecom to discuss your plans and get ideas on the latest equipment.
2. Decide which services you are going to offer. It is possible to offer several different kinds of service at the same time.
3. Contact the sort of businesses who might be interested, and advertise locally.
4. Employ other telephone operators if necessary.

## PROJECT 41: A MAILING LIST BROKER

| | |
|---|---|
| *Status* | Part-time |
| *Capital required* | Low |
| *Return* | High |
| *Can be combined with* | Projects 35, 37 and 38 |

### Project facts
One popular way of promoting a product is by mailshot — the mailing of an attractive sales package to potential buyers. However, such a system has one basic requirement — names and addresses of potential prospects. A thriving mini-industry has developed to supply this need — the mailing list broker.

List brokers buy names and addresses from their sources then hire them out to users of mailshots several times over. The 'buy-in' cost is very little, but the 'rent-out' price is high and is repeatable. Hence there is considerable scope for profit in selling this unusual product.

## What do I need?

- A typewriter.
- Possibly secretarial help.
- Access to a photocopier.
- An accommodation address, if working from home.
- A microcomputer with a mailing list facility for a larger operation.
- The British List Brokers Association, Westbourne Grove, London, W2, could provide useful information.

## Pros and cons

| Pros | Cons |
|---|---|
| You can rent out the same list several times | Competition is strong |
| To start with overheads can be kept very low | Lists need to be updated regularly |

## How do I operate?

The business needs to look professional. You could work at home but if you do, use an accommodation address to promote a professional image. Buy names and addresses by approaching businesses who keep customer lists and asking to buy them (a sample letter is shown on the opposite page). Offer a fee rather than a royalty. Some will not divulge customer names but others will if assured of confidential treatment of these records. For example, a garage business will hold names and addresses of car owners for which you could find a ready market. Pay them 20p per name and they could find the income very useful! Compile these names and addresses into mailing lists, either by computer or typed onto A4 sheets of paper. Give each name a reference number so that you can check how often it is hired out to customers.

Offer the names for sale. The best way to do this is by sending a sales letter to potential users. For example, names of car owners could be sold to insurance companies or motoring clubs. Offer to rent lists out at about £20 per hundred names. Hence, one rental of a name gets your outlay price back. Rent it out four or five times more for your profit.

When customers rent a list, take a printout from the computer or photocopy a typed list. Transfer the list onto adhesive labels in both cases. These can be used on the buyer's mailshot. The idea is that one fee allows the list to be used once only. Repeat use of the list must be paid for again. A good idea is to put a couple of names and addresses of friends or relatives in each list hired. This

**MAILING LIST SERVICES COMPANY**
169 High Street, Anytown. Tel. 789789.

Dear Sirs

How can you make more money from your customers without asking them for a penny more? By 'lending' us their addresses for use in our professional list-broking service!

If you keep records of customers' addresses we may be prepared to buy the use of them from you for a substantial fee! The reason we can afford to do this is that we have considerable demand from respected national companies seeking names and addresses for their mailshot marketing techniques. And we can pay you for supplying us.

Any addresses you might supply us with would be kept confidential at all times, and only used for the purposes of sending tasteful mailings on everyday products and services. Contrary to popular opinion, the vast majority of people don't mind mailings of this kind.

This really can be an excellent way of raising income to improve the service you offer at present for virtually no work or effort on your part.

If you have addresses that may be suitable for our needs please do contact us by return. We shall be pleased to reassure you as to the confidentiality of our service and explain how easily you can turn mere names and addresses into MONEY!

Yours faithfully


for Mailing List Services

Sample letter asking to buy names and addresses

way you can check on use and misuse of the list.

There are many ways of expanding. For example, you can find new lists for past customers, or rerent past lists to new customers (limit the number of times one address is used) until they are about one year old. This system allows you to expand to any level you want. Some brokers have millions of names and addresses in hundreds of customer categories.

## How much can I earn?

**Example:** One small list broker regularly keeps 5,000 'live' addresses. These are bought in for approximately 15p each then rented out five or six times over six months for £22 per hundred. Over six months the full list can produce £6,600, yet it only cost £750 to buy, spread over a period of months. His profit is therefore almost £6,000 in six months, less expenses.

This business only runs part time and has lots of room to expand. It generally buys customer names from newsagents, and then sells them to magazine publishers for promotional mailings. This is just one idea from hundreds of possibilities for types of lists you could handle.

## Summary
1. Your business must look professional.
2. Approach businesses who keep customer lists and ask to buy them. Pay about 20p per name.
3. Compile mailing lists from the names and addresses you have, in categories.
4. Send a sales letter to potential users, offering your list for rent. Charge about £20 per hundred.
5. Provide labels for your customers' mailshots, to prevent them using the names twice. Each subsequent use should be charged again.

---

## PROJECT 42: EDITING AND PROOFREADING

| | |
|---|---|
| *Status* | Part-time only |
| *Capital required* | Very low |
| *Return* | Moderate |
| *Can be combined with* | Projects 71 and 87 |

---

## Project facts
Many businesses exploit a small niche in the market, but which

nevertheless offers an excellent return for the small, efficient business. An author's editing and proofreading service is one such business.

There are thousands and thousands of professional and amateur authors and writers. Most of them prefer writing to reading. This offers scope for someone to read and correct all manner of manuscripts that writers produce.

### What do I need?
- A liking for reading.
- An eye for grammatical and spelling errors, or inconsistencies in a piece of writing.
- The *Writers' and Artists' Yearbook* will provide much valuable information.

### Pros and cons

| Pros | Cons |
|---|---|
| The overheads are minimal | Competition is strong |
| An enjoyable way to earn money if you have wide-ranging tastes in books | from people with professional experience |

### How do I operate?
Your customers are amateur and professional authors and writers. You only need a handful providing work on a regular basis for a satisfactory part-time business.

Advertise thoroughly. This can be done in popular newspapers and magazines likely to attract writers. You may also qualify for an entry in the *Writers' and Artists' Yearbook* (published annually) which is the accepted writers' reference guide. Also get entries in the various media directories — available in your library.

The operation is simple, but involves an aptitude for careful reading. Basically, customers send you their manuscript. It is then your job to check it for errors of any kind. These include grammatical, spelling, typographical and layout errors. You don't correct the errors, merely mark them for the author's attention.

There are standard editors' markings for errors in manuscripts. Details of these can be found in the *Writers' and Artists' Yearbook* which is worth purchasing for this trade. The guide in this book will also tell you what constitutes a manuscript error, as it may not be an error in ordinary writing.

When the manuscript is marked, return it to the author. It is their job to have it retyped, if necessary (and maybe reread) before submission to a publisher. The cost of your service is well worth it — the author has better quality work to submit to his publisher and it may make the difference between speculative work being accepted or rejected. It could also eliminate charges to authors for submitting error-ridden manuscripts.

You could expand into doing similar work for publishers.

## Summary

1. Advertise widely in popular magazines and newspapers.
2. Try to get an entry in the *Writers' and Artists' Yearbook*.
3. When writers send you their manuscripts, check them thoroughly for errors or inconsistencies of any kind.
4. Mark any errors for the writer's attention.

---

## PROJECT 43: A CAR BROKER

| | |
|---|---|
| *Status* | Part-time/full-time |
| *Capital required* | Very low |
| *Return* | Short-term moderate, long-term high. |
| *Can be combined with* | Project 33 |

---

### Project facts

Motor vehicle sales have become increasingly competitive in the past few years, so much so that procuring a discount on a new car is taken for granted. This has opened up an entirely new service, known as car broking.

The car broker offers new vehicles for sale at well below list price. He does this by 'shopping around' a number of appointed dealers for their best 'trade' price. As a result the customer gets a wider choice of vehicles at prices lower than he could negotiate, and the broker claims a commission for himself!

### What do I need?

- Cash for advertising (suggest £250 upwards).
- Small office space at home.
- Telephone.
- Good quality business stationery.
- Good telephone manner and organisational skills.
- Motor trade contacts desirable, but not essential.
- The Motor Manufacturers and Traders Society, Forbes House, Halkin Street, London, SW1X 7DS, is a trade association, although they do not actually represent brokers.

- *What Car?* (available at most newsagents) has advertisements from brokers, so you can see how they operate.

## Pros and cons

| Pros | Cons |
|------|------|
| Low overheads | Some knowledge of the trade desirable |
| Can build up to a high profit level | May take time to build the business up |

### How do I operate?

The business centres around comprehensive advertising. This can be undertaken in local and national newspapers as well as the motoring periodicals (consult *Benn's Media Directory* for details). Ads are placed offering new cars at a discount greater than that offered by a franchised dealer.

When customers respond, the service is explained. Details of the car they require and a contact phone number are taken.

At this point the work begins. Telephone a wide selection of dealers holding the appropriate franchise. Contact them through the Yellow Pages. (Look under **Car Dealers and Distributors.**) Explain that you are a broker. (You must do this or they will probably not negotiate.) State the car model and specification your customer requires and ask for a keen 'on the road' price.

Some negotiating ability is needed here, but the chances are that if they have a suitable vehicle they will quote a price less than the price to a retail customer calling at the showrooms. The reasons for this are various, but centre around oversupply in the industry and sales incentives offered by makers to dealers.

The next step is to communicate this price to the customer, adding a mark-up for yourself. Typically, brokers get a 15% discount on the list price from a dealer and sell on at a 13% discount, thus leaving a good margin, and a good saving for the customer.

If the customer accepts the quote their new vehicle is delivered direct from the supplying dealer. That dealer collects payment and forwards a commission to the broker.

This system is well used within the motor trade and most dealers will cooperate. More lucrative deals can be arranged as knowledge of the motor trade increases.

### How much can I earn?

**Example:** Mr A requires a new Ford. He contacts three dealers in his area, and the cheapest quote they give is £6,925. None of the dealers has a vehicle in stock in Mr A's preferred colours.

Mr A contacts a broker. The broker knows from experience which Ford dealers offer keen prices and good stocks. He rings six nationwide. The best price obtained is £6,095 with vehicles in stock for immediate delivery.

The broker conveys the details to Mr A offering his first colour choice for which the broker charges £6,395. The vehicle is delivered three days later.

In this example the customer makes a good saving (£530) and the broker gets a commission of about £300. This can be increased on more costly cars and repeated several times a week!

## Summary

1. Advertise your service, offering new cars at a substantial discount.
2. When you receive a response, take the details of the car required.
3. Phone a wide selection of dealers nationwide to see whether they have a car of the right specifications, and what discount they are prepared to offer.
4. Quote the price to the customer, adding a mark-up for yourself.
5. The car is delivered direct to the customer by the dealer, who collects payment and forwards your commission.

## PROJECT 44: A USED CAR BROKER

| | |
|---|---|
| *Status* | Part-time, possibly full-time |
| *Capital required* | Very low |
| *Return* | Good |

### In brief

Another useful service for the motor trade is ideal as a part-time home business needing no significant capital. That is a broking service for second-hand used cars.

Most motor traders make good profits on dealing in used cars and are always anxious to offer the most suitable and profitable vehicles. Demand varies from area to area and vehicles which sell poorly at one garage are in great demand at another.

This opens up potential for a broker's register of used cars to be established. Quite simply, you would write to garages large and small explaining the concept of your service. Charge them an annual fee of £100 – £200 to register with you. Each month, they would send you a list of used cars they are willing to trade with other garages. You publish this as a 'digest' and mail a copy to all other member garages.

Dealers can then contact each other to buy, sell or exchange vehicles in order to give their customers the best selection at the best profits. So, for example, a Ford dealer might exchange a Mercedes car he has taken in part-exchange for two Fords held by a Mercedes dealer. Both dealers can then sell cars of their own particular make at better prices than an 'outside' make.

Make contacts through the Yellow Pages nationwide or possibly use a guide like the Automobile Association (AA) or Royal Automobile Club (RAC) handbooks, which can be bought direct from these organisations.

Further details on how to proceed will be found in **Project 43.**

---

## PROJECT 45: A FREE NEWSPAPER

| | |
|---|---|
| *Status* | Mostly full-time |
| *Capital required* | High |
| *Return* | High, long-term |
| *Can be combined with* | Projects 2, 32, 46 and 71 |

---

### Project facts

There can be very few businesses which give their product away free, and still make money, but there is one excellent example — the free newspaper. There is scope for expansion in this area, and it is quite possible to start from scratch given a moderate amount of capital — £1,000 upwards is suggested as being sufficient for the most basic operation.

Of course, a free newspaper sells advertising, not itself, and being free provides an attractive way of exploiting the need of advertisers to make their products more widely known. Though many free newspapers do exist already, the busier areas can support more. One way of finding a lucrative niche is to make your new free paper specialist, for example serving only large modern estates, or areas of volume housing like flats. This can often appeal to advertisers because it allows them to target their advertising accurately.

## What do I need?

- A source of local news to give the paper reader appeal. Retain a part-time journalist or use a freelance.
- Advertising sales staff to get advertising from trade and private customers. The main requirement here is a room with two or three phones and telephone sales staff (part-time if necessary). Advertise for all your staff in local papers or through Job Centres. Do note that it is best to employ experienced, specialist telesales staff. This form of selling is quite specialised and it is better to use the ready-made skills of suitable staff than to try and train those who are not experienced.
- Typesetting and printing facilities. Look under **Typesetters** and **Printers** in the Yellow Pages.
- A distribution network. Use a leaflet distribution firm — look under **Circular and Sample Distributors** in the Yellow Pages.

## Pros and cons

| Pros | Cons |
|---|---|
| Substantial, regular takings once established | High investment needed (even a relatively large amount will finance only a modest project) |
| The business generally is a growth area | You will enter quite a competitive industry |

## How do I operate?

The object of the business is to produce a newspaper funded by advertising for free door-to-door distribution. This could start from home, but a small front office in a city or town centre is ideal.

One difficult point is getting a first issue out when advertisers have yet to see the paper. The solution is to produce a pilot issue, possibly giving advertisers free space, then distributing more copies than you expect to distribute free in future. This is a good way of creating an impact and getting good results for your advertisers in order to get subsequent business!

Another problem can be cash flow. Since trade advertising is traditionally sold on 30 day credit terms you must monitor this carefully to ensure you are paid promptly. The use of a credit collection agency to monitor and collect accounts will save on internal administration.

After the initial test issue the procedure is very much the same, publishing on a weekly basis (or preferably fortnightly initially):

1.  Advertising sales staff canvass business customers to buy ad

space. The public phone or post their classified ads.
2. The reporter submits local news.
3. The editor (either yourself or an employee) selects the required material and sends it with a rough layout to the printers or typesetters.
4. The newspaper is typeset, printed, and forwarded direct to the distributors.
5. The distributors drop copies door-to-door in the required area.

You can expand by increasing the distribution, thus attracting more advertisers seeking a wider readership. This in turn should appeal to more readers with a resultant rise in the response rate.

Ideally, an operator of this business should only expect to cover his costs in the first six months or so. There is even potential to test the idea in several different areas to see where the best profits can be had. Once established though, returns can be considerable. A typical 'mini' paper might take £18,000 in advertising revenue per issue, yet cost about £4,000 to print and distribute (excluding other costs).

*Important Note:* The nature of this business is too specialist for the owner to undertake all the functions. It does require the retention of experienced staff. However, it also offers scope for a start-up opportunity for the more determined newcomer. A pilot issue could be launched for a fraction of the usual cost, then used as a springboard to attract advertising custom.

## Summary
1. You will need specialist staff.
2. Print a pilot issue first to test the market and attract advertisers.
3. Employ advertising sales staff to get advertisers.
4. Employ a reporter (possibly freelance) to provide news.
5. When all the advertising and news is in, make a rough layout and send it to the typesetter or printer.
6. The printer sends the finished newspaper direct to the distributor.

# PROJECT 46: A MINI ADVERTISING AGENCY

| | |
|---|---|
| *Status* | Mostly full-time |
| *Capital required* | Ideally high |
| *Return* | Good |
| *Can be combined with* | Projects 2 and 89 |

## Project facts

Advertising is vital to any business. It has become big business itself by way of the advertising agency. Ad agencies take control of all publicity for a client and ensure it is professional, so it is the ideal type of activity for someone with good organisational skills.

Most agencies deal only with clients spending tens of thousands and more on advertising in a year. So there are openings to provide a service to smaller businesses — those who only spend thousands. Because it is smaller, it is an area newcomers can operate in.

## What do I need?

To start, you will need:

- A visualiser, to produce illustrations (it is good if they are also a graphic artist and/or a photographer).
- A copywriter, to produce ad copy.
- A professional print and media buyer, to liaise with printers and sources of advertising.
- An account executive, to get customers and liaise between customers and these specialists. You could do this yourself.
- The professional associations are the Advertising Association, 15 Wilton Road, London SW1V 1NJ, and the Institute of Practitioners in Advertising, 44 Belgrave Square, London SW1X 8QS.
- The Advertising Standards Authority, 2–16 Torrington Place, London WC1E 7HN, provides information on the legal requirements for advertising.
- The trade journals are *Campaign* and *Marketing,* also the *Advertiser's Annual* (available at main libraries). Any main library will also stock a number of press and media guides through which suppliers of services such as copywriting and design can be found. Use the Yellow Pages for possible customer leads.
- One of the few readily understandable books on advertising

technique is *Do Your Own Advertising* by Alastair Crompton, published by Hutchinson (1986).

The business can be based at home, or a small office in a professional area can 'front' the business, with all your part-time professionals working from home alongside other jobs.

## Pros and cons

| Pros | Cons |
|---|---|
| Advertising is a major growth industry | You are reliant on 'outside' staff |
| Eventually, order values can reach into hundreds of thousands of pounds | Very competitive once you start aiming for larger accounts |
| | The capital injection may need to be high for the business to develop successfully |

## How do I operate?

Most businesses need professional advertising advice, but a good start into the market is to approach small firms who have not used ad agencies before. Look at companies with a turnover of less than £1,000,000 for good prospects.

The idea of your service is to take over their advertising needs from them, and with professional handling to get better results. This saves them money by more skilful use of advertising capital. So, for example, you will arrange drawing up, copywriting and insertion of all their press ads, or the writing and printing of any brochures or leaflets they need.

Sell to possible customers in person. The Yellow Pages is also a good source of contacts for this activity. The easiest way of charging when you start off is on a percentage basis. For example, if you place £5,000 worth of press advertisements for a customer your charge might be 10% or 25% of that amount plus any design or writing costs.

At the start of an arrangement sit down with each customer and plan their advertising needs for the next twelve months. Ascertain what results they expect and what they want to spend. Draw up your proposals for a one-year advertising campaign. Consult with your retained advisers to arrange this. Present and agree the campaign with the client. For example, you might decide on a press campaign from January to April, mailshots in May and June, then a new press campaign running up to Christmas.

As each job becomes due you plan and arrange the necessary

work. For example, for a press ad:

— The account executive gets details of the latest product from customer.
— He asks the visualiser to produce a page layout.
— He asks the copywriter to do the wording.
— He agrees this with the customer.
— He gets the media buyer to negotiate and book space in newspapers on the keenest possible terms and perhaps gets the print buyer to negotiate with a printer to print copies of the ad for use as leaflets. Then he gets them distributed door-to-door.

The result of a well-planned campaign is better-looking advertising and, more than likely, a better response for the customer than 'DIY' advertising. For a typical small business the agency could, perhaps, handle £20,000 of advertising, claiming commission of £4,000 or so for their own services.

Repeat this process throughout the year for each client, aiming to get the best results for each advertising pound they spend. Renegotiate the contract annually or, once established, five-yearly. A number of accounts can be handled at the same time for considerable annual commission.

## Summary
1. You will need a number of professionals (designers, copywriters etc) working for you on a freelance basis.
2. Sell to possible customers on a personal basis. Look for customers with a turnover of less than a million pounds.
3. Plan a year's campaign with the customer.
4. As each stage in the campaign becomes due, get details of the customer's product, get the visualiser to produce a layout and the copywriter to write the copy for each publicity piece.
5. Agree these with the customer, and get the media buyer to book space, or the print buyer to negotiate the printing of a leaflet.

# PROJECT 47: TOURS AND EXCURSIONS

| | |
|---|---|
| *Status* | Part-time/full-time/occasional |
| *Capital required* | High |
| *Return* | High, fast |
| *Can be combined with* | Projects 7, 22, 72 and 95 |

## Project facts

Tourism is a huge industry which involves national companies. But there are opportunities for small, local companies to enter the market producing carefully organised trips and tours for personal, individual needs.

If you have an interest in people and places then you can plan, organise and conduct these excursions. Apart from anything else this could be the forerunner to a much larger business.

## What do I need?

- Capital to support planning and advertising.
- Good organisational ability.
- A small office.
- A good selection of travel guide books.
- The Association of British Travel Agents (ABTA), 55–57 Newman St, London W1P 4AH, will provide professional assistance for travel agent members.
- The British Tourist Authority, Thames Tower, Black's Road, London W6 9EL (Tel.01-846 9000), will provide information.
- Any main library (periodical or reference section) will contain a range of travel trade and tourist guides and journals which will be of help in planning, booking and promoting tours.
  Try *Travel Trade Directory, Owen's Business Directory and Travel Guide, RAC Guide and Handbook, Good Hotel Guide.*
- *The Traveller* (a quarterly journal for overseas travellers) would be of some use in this business.

## Pros and cons

| Pros | Cons |
|---|---|
| Can be fun if you like people and places | Could be competition from established operators |
| High return | High initial cost |
| Travel and tourism is a growth area | Needs good organisational ability |

## How do I operate?

It is better to begin as a tour operator in a modest way but to offer an individual personal service as an alternative to the 'package deals' of the big companies. To avoid 'red tape' begin by only offering UK tours.

You'll need to think of a tour theme that will attract interest. Take a look in magazines to get some ideas. Try and aim for a specialist need, for example, pensioners' spring breaks at the coast, skiing in a little-known resort, or a break in a remote castle.

Decide the nature of the tour. It might be just a single day, a weekend, a long weekend (4 days), a week or two weeks. Long weekends and full weeks are probably best to start. Write down a 'tour profile' explaining the concept of the trip, the things you want to include and the experiences you want people to have.

The next step is to sit down with a telephone and telephone directories. Make some enquires and get things organised. Any tour has three main components:

1. Transport. Will you provide transport or do customers get there themselves? If you are providing it, contact coach companies for quotes for a coach there and back.
2. Accommodation. Will it be a hotel, a guest house, tents, some special accommodation like a castle or just a day trip? Contact the appropriate sources and get several quotes. Be sure of what you are being offered, eg twin rooms with *en suite* bath, evening meal and breakfast in the case of a hotel.
3. Activities. Most tours will include some organised and/or optional activities or excursions, such as a circus, a local historic site, or an evening dance in the hotel. Find out the additional costs (if any).

At this point you will have various cost options from which you can plan your tour and ultimately work out the customer cost. Facilities will also need to be booked at this stage, and some deposit will need to be paid. Try to get suppliers to give you a provisional booking for, say, 30 days. This holds open the option to cancel if the tour fails to sell.

A good trip will need some sales literature. For major excursions this could be a glossy colour brochure — contact a design and print firm for this. For smaller 'start-up' trips it could be far simpler, perhaps a two-colour leaflet illustrated with snapshots of the tour — contact a general printer. Order quantities according to how you will send them out — whether through travel agents or in response to personal enquiries.

It is quite possible to sell the tour yourself, from home, but you will need to take sufficient space in the local press, illustrated where possible, to gain interest. Take telephone enquiries for brochures and accept bookings by phone with payment to follow.

An easier way to sell is to ask a travel agent to handle this. Pay them on commission of about 10% or 12%. Apart from your press advertising they can advertise in their shop, and they may have contacts with other agents in other areas. They can handle all enquiries, bookings and payments very professionally.

Overall expect about 15% – 20% of enquiries to convert into bookings. As a consequence there should always be an option to cancel the tour if bookings are poor. Similarly, there should be scope to add duplicate tours if they are popular.

There is a good deal of office administration in any trip. In the first instance you will need to take payments from customers before the departure date. Then you will have to pay the bills for transport, accommodation and facilities — if possible arrange to pay most of these costs after the trip.

The actual organisation of the trip is rather easier and can be conducted personally. Alternatively, you can engage travel couriers whose job is to follow the programme you have set, and smooth out any problems that occur.

The best way of expanding is with repeat business — getting the same customers to travel with you regularly. An obvious way is to organise more regular tours or try branching out into different subjects and regions. Another way to expand is by running overseas tours. You may need licences and the best way to overcome this is to cooperate with an established travel agent. Remember though, this area is much more competitive.

Bear in mind the following points:

— Watch the cost of the 'components' of the tour and hence the overall price. Do not exceed 'average' prices.
— Get written confirmation of all bookings and prices.
— Avoid using customers' deposits to pay advance costs as this can lead to cash flow difficulties.
— Arrange insurance for accidents or the cancellation of the tour, as well as insurance to safeguard customer payments in case your arrangements fail (for example, if the coach operator goes bankrupt).

## How much can I earn?

**Example:** A tour operator organises a three-day 'singles' tour to the Lake District. He offers places at £119, and attracts 55 clients. His revenue is £6,545.

| | |
|---|---|
| Coach transport | £420 |
| Hotel accommodation for two nights B&B | £1,175 |
| Gala dinner at restaurant on first evening | £460 |
| Patio barbecue second evening | £260 |
| Excursion Day 1, Boat trip Day 2 | £110 |
| Picnic lunches three days | £260 |
| Advertising in regional paper and other administrative expenses | £1,110 |
| Services of freelance guide | £270 |
| Total Costs | £4,065 |
| Total Revenue | £6,545 |
| Profit (excluding some minor expenses) | £2,480 |

## Summary

1. Start in a small way, and stick to the UK initially.
2. Find a theme for your tour.
3. Decide on the length of the tour.
4. Organise transport, hotels and activities, and try to get provisional bookings initially.
5. Produce a brochure, and advertise in the press, as well as selling through travel agents.
6. Organise the collection of payments and the settling of bills with coach operator, hotels etc.
7. It is best to arrange insurance, in case things go wrong.

---

## PROJECT 48: PARTY ORGANISATION

| | |
|---|---|
| *Status* | Mostly part-time, can be full-time |
| *Capital required* | Low |
| *Return* | Good, occasional |
| *Can be combined with* | Projects 46 and 59 |

---

## Project facts

Leisure activities are becoming ever more popular, and so are the businesses surrounding them. Of these, one business with the greatest potential is in professional party organisation, whether for special family occasions or corporate functions.

An enjoyable party needs to be properly planned. There are

now services which offer to do this for the exclusive party-holder who is prepared to pay. The service is popular in major cities, but scope exists in busier provincial towns and cities.

Typically, you act as just an organiser, working on your telephone to bring together all the important threads from other suppliers. You charge your own fee and perhaps claim commission on the services of others. Of course, customers for such a service are limited, but the fees charged (£500 – £5,000 per party) mean you only need a commission now and then to succeed.

## What do I need?
- A telephone.
- First-class organisational ability.
- A supply of Yellow Pages to find the suppliers you need.
- There are many books on party catering. One is Prue Leith's *Dinner Parties,* published by Robert Hale (1984).

## Pros and cons

| Pros | Cons |
| --- | --- |
| Profits can be high | Requires a lot of organisation |
| It is a growth area | Limited demand at present |

## How do I operate?
Start off by advertising in quality regional newspapers and county magazines. You're aiming for exclusive parties and ordinary newspapers, leaflets etc just won't do. The bulk of your business will come by word of mouth once started. There isn't any substitute for this.

Visit enquirers in person. Quote a fully inclusive price for a complete party concept. Base this on your costs to organise plus a 20% – 40% margin. Bear in mind the price guide above and always charge more rather than less!

Once a quote is accepted discuss plans carefully with the client. Determine what sort of party they require, what sort of theme, what sort of atmosphere is required. You'll almost always find a client wants to give a particular impression to guests — and everything you organise should fit within the theme.

It is your job to book the suppliers of party services, having first checked out exactly what is required with the client. You may be required to organise a function suite, a night club, a marquee, the client's home or an unusual venue like a boat or a train; handle administration, like printing and posting of invitations; book a band, disco or other entertainers; organise food and drink, either with the function suite or with outside caterers; organise decor, flowers etc with an interior designer or florist; organise security and hostesses to supervise, and someone to handle unforeseen problems; or organise chauffeur-driven transport for client and important guests.

There will be other jobs according to the particular party, but this framework covers the main items. Although some appear straightforward many are very complicated. For more exclusive party-holders your service will be cheap even at hundreds or thousands of pounds.

### How much can I earn?

**Example:** One party organiser planned an exclusive 40th birthday party for a wealthy train enthusiast. He hired a steam locomotive from one of the private railways and four vintage carriages. Guests ate and drank as the train ran across bleak moorland. 'Breaking down' at a deserted and supposedly haunted station was a surprise prank planned as an extra service! The event cost about £1,800 to organise and the organiser charged £2,595.

**Example:** A surprise wedding reception for two potholing enthusiasts held in an illuminated, decorated and heated cave (a pothole was just that bit too small!) cost £600 to arrange. The organiser charged double that.

### Summary
1. Advertise in quality regional newspapers and county magazines.
2. Visit enquirers in person to establish their needs.
3. Book the suppliers of the party services you need.
4. Charge according to the service, but typically between £500 and £5,000.

## PROJECT 49: ART SALES

| | |
|---|---|
| *Status* | Part-time only |
| *Capital required* | Moderate |
| *Return* | Good, occasional |
| *Can be combined with* | Project 62 |

### Project facts
The majority of *retail* businesses need a shop, or at least a stall.

Not many can be genuinely operated from the comfort of home. However, here is one that can be — selling oil paintings. Because art offers a high profit margin it can profitably be sold at home, even though individual sales may be few. It requires only a little organisation and will not intrude unnecessarily into the home.

## What do I need?
- Space to display paintings.
- A source of supply.
- Some knowledge of art is an advantage.

## Pros and cons

| Pros | Cons |
|---|---|
| Overheads are very small | The size of the business is limited to space at home |
| Oil paintings are presently a 'growth market' | Could disrupt home life to some extent |

## How do I operate?
Choose and buy 6 – 12 original oil paintings. There are several suppliers of inexpensive imported paintings. They advertise in Sunday newspapers and magazines like *Exchange & Mart*. Have them framed by a local framer, or do it yourself.

Display the paintings around your home. A spare bedroom, dining room or the hall, stairs and landing are ideal. Redecorate these areas to complement the paintings if necessary.

Advertise your 'home gallery' in the local press. Give only a telephone number so that interested parties must telephone to make an appointment to view. Art lovers visit your home, by arrangement, to view the paintings in comfort. In such surroundings about 80% of visits could result in a sale. The best picture prices are around £30 – £250 each.

This business offers many opportunities for expansion. Consider renting a corner of another shop to set up a gallery display, or open up a small painting gallery of your own. Old, run-down 'character' premises are perfectly suitable.

## How much can I earn?
A typical 18in x 24in oil painting on canvas could be bought for about £8 from a wholesale painting importer. The costs of framing this in a mid-quality frame at a framing service would be about £15. Hence your typical product cost is £23. Sale prices very much depend on the quality of the work, but this sort of painting could

easily sell for £80, giving you a gross profit of around £57.

This kind of service might sell two or three paintings a week. Don't expect any more than this for a small operation. However, even one weekly sale offers a good income.

## Summary

1. This is a very easy operation to run.
2. Buy a few paintings from an importer.
3. Have them framed.
4. Advertise your service locally. Only give a telephone number to prevent casual callers.
5. If you decide to expand, you can rent space in a shop.

---

# PROJECT 50: BARTER

| | |
|---|---|
| *Status* | Usually part-time |
| *Capital required* | None |
| *Return* | Very high, but uncertain |
| *Can be combined with* | Projects 25 and 26 |

---

## Project facts

Most businesses buy and sell something, but it doesn't have to be that way. There is potential to exchange (or barter) your way to a considerable portfolio of possessions and finances. A number of wealthy people run no particular business, but amass their income through 'swapping' things with other people.

Barter is an ancient form of trading and works because different things have different values to different people. So you can barter one thing to an eager 'buyer' for more than you could sell it for, in exchanged goods. This is not a business as such, but is a good way of making money that is more attractive than it might seem.

## What do I need?

● Something to barter.

## Pros and cons

| Pros | Cons |
|---|---|
| No capital is needed to start | No guaranteed income possible |
| | Money can very easily be lost as well as gained |

## How do I operate?

Your initial item for barter could be a car, valuable jewellery, property, or perhaps just a TV set. Advertise your barter in local and national newspapers. A few have specialist columns. *Exchange & Mart* is often used by barterers. Describe your barter and put 'will exchange for why'. 'Why' means 'what have you' — in barterers' terms it could be anything!

Wait for offers. When you receive a suitable one exchange the item for anything you consider to be more valuable. Repeat the process continually.

Sell bartered goods from time to time for an income. Others remain your stock for continual barter for more valuable items. For example a barterer may exchange his Ford car for some jewellery. He gets this for less than cash value because the seller urgently needs transport and has no cash. The barterer then sells some of this for income, but barters the rest for a small apartment in Spain. He may rent out the apartment for a year for income, then exchange it for a boat and a Mercedes car. The boat is then bartered for a small grocery business. This business is expanded and later bartered for a country cottage.

The barterer in question neither needs nor wants many of these items. But because others want what he has more than what they exchange, he can increase the value of his assets step by step — often without running a conventional business!

## Summary

1. Advertise your item for barter.
2. When someone responds with an item you think is more valuable, exchange items.
3. Keep exchanging, occasionally selling items for income.

# PROJECT FILE 3
## Practical Businesses

These are businesses which involve manual activity —
making or repairing, or providing a manual service. They
will therefore appeal to people who dislike a lot of
paperwork and administration. Some manual ability may
be involved in some of the projects, but there are others
where no great skill is required.

## PROJECT 51: REPLACEMENT KITCHEN DOORS AND DRAWERS

| | |
|---|---|
| *Status* | Part-time/full-time |
| *Capital required* | High |
| *Return* | High, long-term |
| *Can be combined with* | Project 81 |

### Project facts

Home improvements are big business and one type always leads the list for consumer spending — new kitchens.

The appeal is to the more affluent market sectors. There are already many operators in the trade, but this project is a reasonably new service and operates on a more cost-effective basis, so it is set to grow fast over coming years.

The business is in replacement kitchen doors, drawer fronts and work surfaces, a business that is so effective and yet ridiculously simple — you can open one day and trade the next.

### What do I need?

- A supply of ready-made kitchen doors and drawers, and work-top materials.
- An ability to deal with the public.
- Some practical skills.
- Transport.
- A small showroom to display products — or you could work from home.
- Capital for advertising.
- Competent joiners to fit new doors.
- Useful contacts could be tracked down through woodworking journals such as *Woodworker* or *Woodworking Crafts,* available at main libraries. Magazines such as *Ideal Home* and *Homes and Gardens* could be useful for interior design information.
- The appropriate trade bodies are the Kitchen Specialists Association, 31 Bois Lane, Chesham Bois, Amersham, Buckinghamshire (Tel. (0403) 41259) and, to some extent, the Bathroom and Shower Centre, 204 Great Portland Street, London W1N 6AT (Tel.01-388 7631).

## Pros and cons

**Pros**
This is a growth area
Profits can be high

**Cons**
Requires fairly high investment
Can take some time to
become established

## How do I operate?

First find a supplier of new kitchen doors and drawer fronts.
There are a number of specialist manufacturing joiners. Look
under **Joinery Manufacturers** in the Yellow Pages nationally.
Alternatively, you could contact a competent local joiner and ask
him to quote for making new doors and drawer fronts to measure.

You don't need to hold stocks, just contact your suppliers as you
receive orders. However, most kitchen units are a standard size so
you could take stocks of the necessary parts and fit them to a high
standard with only minor modifications.

Check with existing kitchen centres to see what materials
are in fashion. Woods like pine, cherry, walnut and oak are
popular. Smooth laminates are always in demand, though designs
and colours can change annually. To start successfully you would
probably need to offer a choice of 5 – 8 different replacement
materials.

Another important contact is a joiner to fit new items for
you (unless you have a leaning for DIY). Make sure you find
someone who can handle this type of work. You could employ
self-employed joiners, or joiners working for larger firms who will
work for you outside working hours. Talented DIY buffs might
be suitable. Advertise through Job Centres and in the local press.
Engage part-time staff and pay by the hour.

Once you have your materials and workforce lined up it is
a good idea to test the arrangement. You could refit your own
kitchen, and use it as a display, or fit out a showroom (rent a
town centre shop).

You then need something else to show prospective customers.
A showroom with displays is fine, but it is even better to
have coloured particulars showing the various alternatives and
combinations. Brochures are essential if you have no showroom.
Often the product manufacturers can supply these or you can make
up your own. A freelance photographer, writer and colour printer
should be able to help. You should also have samples of the various
materials you offer.

Next, advertise the service using local press ads (take full or

---

half pages if possible), door-to-door leaflets, and door-to-door calling.

Keep your sales effort quite separate from the new kitchen activities of other companies. Remember, you are selling and fitting new kitchen doors, drawer fronts and work surfaces only onto existing 'carcasses' in existing fitted kitchens. Such a service costs only about half as much as all-new units, so you are aiming at a much cheaper market. Thousands of people could not afford (or would not want to spend money on) a whole new kitchen but would be interested in this facility.

Those who show an interest should be visited personally for the service to be explained and brochures and samples shown. Work out the new items needed, their cost to you, then add a mark-up (about 150%) to cover fitting and your profit. This forms a speedy 'free quotation' for the enquirer's attention.

Once a customer places an order, take a 50% deposit. Send the joiners to measure the size of existing cupboard doors, drawer fronts and work surfaces, forward the details to the manufacturers and instruct them to make replacements to the same size in the chosen material. When they are available, arrange a fitting date with all parties. The joiners fit the new items, and you call to check the work — and collect the balance!

Most re-fit services end there, but there is extra potential to provide other interior decorating services such as painting to complete the room setting for lucrative extra income.

The actual refurbishment may take time to learn at first. However, your eventual aim should be to find reliable staff who can work unsupervised to a high standard, leaving most of your time to administer the sales drive.

**How much can I earn?**
**Example:** One 'kitchen rejuvenation' service charges about £475 to replace doors, drawers and work surfaces in a typical kitchen, that is, an 8ft x 10ft room with fitted cupboards all round.

Of this the new parts and fixings cost around £120. A day's labour takes the costs to £180. Transport and other sundries make the total cost about £200. The remaining balance is profit, less the costs of advertising and selling.

**Summary**
1. Find a source of replacement doors, drawer fronts and work surfaces.
2. Find a good joiner.

3. Advertise through the press, by leafleting and door-to-door calling.
4. When a customer places an order, take a deposit and order the items to his specification.
5. The work needs to be of a high standard to ensure repeat and 'recommendation' orders.

## PROJECT 52: HOME IMPROVEMENTS

| | |
|---|---|
| *Status* | Part-time/full-time |
| *Capital required* | Moderate to high |
| *Return* | High, longer-term |

### In brief
Home improvements are generally big business, and there is always room for honest, competent traders who can market the service in an imaginative way. Two other services can be operated, apart from the kitchen renovation business.

1. Bedrooms. The trend for fitted kitchens has spread into bedrooms. Fitted furniture (wardrobes, drawers, dressing tables etc) is extremely popular and also a prime means of adding value to a home. Concentrate on sales as much as possible. Supplies can be made to measure by specialist joiners, or bought as self-assembly packs from large retailers in most towns.

2. Bathrooms. Cold, stark bathrooms are no longer desirable and comfortable 'luxury' bathrooms are in vogue. Sell imaginatively. Fittings are readily available from plumbers' merchants for fitting by a local plumber.

With both of these the accent is very much on imaginative selling. Design and fitting is less crucial and often handled by subcontractors. You can combine kitchens, bathrooms and bedrooms for a very comprehensive interior refurbishment service!

Further details on how to proceed can be found in **Project 51**.

# PROJECT 53: TELEPHONE FITTING

| | |
|---|---|
| *Status* | Part-time/full-time |
| *Capital required* | Moderate |
| *Return* | Moderate |
| *Can be combined with* | Project 70 |

## Project facts

The growth in the use of telephones in recent years has resulted in great changes in the system. Telephone equipment may now be sold and fitted by any competent person, not just British Telecom personnel. As a result, there are now many private firms offering an alternative to the major companies for the supply and fitting of equipment.

## What do I need?

- Basic knowledge of DIY.
- The *Telecommunications Products and Services Directory*, edited by Michael Corby and published by the Telecommunications Press every two years, is a good source of information.
- *Exchange & Mart* and *Industrial Exchange & Mart* contain advertisements for equipment suppliers.

## Pros and cons

| Pros | Cons |
|---|---|
| Telecommunications is a massive growth industry | Competition is developing quite quickly |
| DIY skill is quite sufficient | |

## How do I operate?

First, check the current regulations on competition. Private companies in the UK are now allowed to offer many of the equipment supply and fitting services previously offered by British Telecom (BT). But do check the current position.

The easiest service to offer is the supply and wiring of domestic telephones. Under present regulations anybody can wire and supply an internal telephone system — so long as the premises are equipped with a plug-in socket already fitted by BT.

Find a supplier of telephone equipment. There are many importers and wholesalers supplying inexpensive imported equipment to appeal to the mass market. Many advertise in the Yellow Pages (look under **Telephone Equipment Manufacturers**) or *Exchange &*

*Mart* available weekly at newsagents. Any equipment you connect to the BT system must be approved for use by BT. Suitable equipment will be marked with a tag or sticker to this effect.

Next, your service should be advertised. Use the local press, but door-to-door leaflets and calling are also effective. A good service to offer householders is a second (or third) telephone, with extension sockets in every room of the house.

The fitting of such a system needs no special skills. DIY enthusiasts can be employed to fit equipment using the simple instructions that should accompany it.

At £50 – £100 for wiring an average house with extensions (excluding new telephones), such a service compares favourably with the competition. So it offers considerable scope for gaining many hundreds of thousands of customers nationwide!

A major advantage of the service is that customers reuse it regularly for alterations and additions to their home telephone systems. There are many further opportunities, such as advanced telephones, like those with 'memory banks', complex business telephone systems, answering machines and facsimile machines, private telephone exchanges, security intercoms or car and portable telephones. All these can be investigated once you start in the business using the contacts you will gain. But a simple home extension service is the place to start.

## How much can I earn?
**Example:** One new company charges £25 to fit a telephone extension socket. The materials for this cost £4.50 and the work takes no more than an hour. They fit four or five per week and get many follow-up orders for other telephone equipment. This is only a tiny business — it could be several times larger.

## Summary
1. Check the current regulations before you start.
2. Find a source of supply.
3. Advertise your service through the press, leafleting and door-to-door calling.
4. You can charge £50 – £100 for wiring an average house with extensions.
5. Once in business, you can start fitting more sophisticated equipment.

## PROJECT 54: FOIL PRINTING

| | |
|---|---|
| *Status* | Mostly part-time |
| *Capital required* | Moderate to high |
| *Return* | Excellent long-term |
| *Can be combined with* | Projects 86, 87, 88 and 89 |

### Project facts

Businesses which combine two popular ideas are usually success-ful, and one which does is the printing of promotional items. On the one hand you are dealing in printing, on the other advertising, hence special opportunities are on offer. One tried and tested way is with hot foil printing. The only special requirement is a purpose-made machine which can produce a wide range of attractive items to sell at attractive prices.

### What do I need?

- A hot foil printing machine. These are frequently advertised in newspapers' 'business' sections and *Exchange & Mart*. At the time of writing prices range from approximately £400 up to several thousands of pounds for the more advanced machines.
- Training — available from specialist suppliers.

### Pros and cons

| Pros | Cons |
|---|---|
| You can build a considerable business on repeat orders | The start-up cost is quite high for a modest income initially |
| The service can be marketed in many different ways | The work is labour intensive |

### How do I operate?

A hot foil printing machine stamps hot type through a roll of foil to emboss items like pens, diaries and business cards. Your service should therefore be advertised to business users. The best way is by personal call. Clubs or societies are also a good sales prospect and some gift shops sell personalised items.

You can offer a wide range of products. Ballpoint pens are a must, but diaries, cards, labels or stickers and leather items like bookmarks can also be offered. Items are bought wholesale, embossed with the machine according to the wording required, and then despatched to your customer. Price your goods at the cost of materials plus around 50% profit margin.

With this business you can undertake both small and large jobs for good profits. However, one of the biggest advantages is that satisfied customers will repeat orders regularly. And the repeat orders offer especially high profit margins once all the initial selling is done.

## How much can I earn?

One part-time foil printer reports sales of £150 - £200 in a typical week, while another outfit which offers all types of promotional products (not just foil printing) expects an annual turnover of £180,000 from their service.

## Summary

1. You will need a hot foil printing machine and some training in using it.
2. Advertise your service by calling. Your customers will be business users, clubs and societies, and perhaps gift shops.
3. You can offer a wide range of products bought wholesale and embossed to order.

---

# PROJECT 55: NATURAL COSMETICS

| | |
|---|---|
| *Status* | Part-time/full-time |
| *Capital required* | Moderate to high |
| *Return* | High in long-term |
| *Can be combined with* | Projects 57 and 60 |

---

## Project facts

Natural products are much in vogue, as buyers turn away from those conintaing harmful chemicals, or tested on animals. This is particularly true for cosmetics. Because natural cosmetics need to be produced on a small scale, this forms an ideal small manufacturing business. Imagination is a great boon.

## What do I need?

- Capital for research and advertising (£500 or more).
- Working space — can operate from home or a small workshop.
- A supply of basic equipment and materials.
- Recipes — can be obtained from health care books.
- Interest in marketing.
- Transport.

- A telephone.
- A small office set-up.
- The relevant trade journals include *Manufacturing Chemist, Soap, Perfumery and Cosmetics* and *Cosmetic World News*. An annual reference book is *Chemist and Druggist Directory*. All are available at main libraries.
- Journals covering health and beauty may be of general interest. Refer to back copies of the women's magazines, and *Here's Health*.

## Pros and cons

| Pros | Cons |
|---|---|
| Can be a very lucrative and attractive modern venture | Capital needed for research and promotion |
| | May take several months to devise and break even |

## How do I operate?

The first essential requirement is to obtain recipes for natural cosmetics. Any modern health care book will help here. Look up the formulae for cosmetic products which use natural ingredients such as herbs, spices and natural oils. There are many products to choose from, including perfumes, aftershaves, *pot-pourri*, cleansing creams, moisturisers, face packs, hair colourings and many others. Select a range of about four or five to start with.

Next, try making up recipes. Use only natural ingredients and pay great attention to cleanliness. Most of the ingredients needed will be found at health food wholesalers or wholesale chemists. (Look under **Chemists: Wholesale** in the Yellow Pages.) All you need is basic kitchen equipment — saucepans, spoons, mixing bowls, a cooker and a fridge. You can obtain this at kitchen discount shops.

Most cosmetic manufacturing procedures are simple. They involve accurate mixing, measuring, heating, filtering and the like. As long as instructions are followed exactly, useable products can be made.

Test your new product range personally, or ask people to use and test them for you as a trial. As long as you have used only safe ingredients, approved by reliable books, there is little danger, but this type of product should always be sold with a reminder to exercise care in use.

Selling the product can be handled initially by you. If the product takes off a marketing agency may be a help.

Products should always be packed in attractive containers, though natural products often sell well in simple ones. There are firms specialising in supplying containers, as well as labels for them. Like all cosmetic products, some sales literature (produced by an advertising copywriter and freelance photographer) will help at the point of sale.

With samples and sales literature available you can start selling. Bear in mind that natural cosmetics won't compete with the international names, at least in the initial stages. Some good sales outlets are:

— Home party plans, or party planners.
— Mail order in health, fashion and beauty magazines.
— Arts and crafts fairs.
— Door-to-door (appoint agents to sell to customers in their neighbourhood).
— Health food or fashion shops locally.
— Beauty salons and health clubs locally.
— Independent local chemists' shops.

Many natural cosmetics products will continue to sell in a small, individual way. Quality products produced in low volume will always sell at high prices to a small, exclusive clientele. There are, however, opportunities to develop into high-volume sales in future by selling to store chains.

## Summary
1. Produce natural products only.
2. Use established recipes (from health care books).
3. Always produce on an individual basis.
4. Be extremely accurate and clean.
5. Sell to special outlets, rather than trying to compete with existing cosmetics companies.

---

# PROJECT 56: NATURAL FOOD

| | |
|---|---|
| *Status* | Part-time/full-time |
| *Capital required* | Moderate (could be high) |
| *Return* | Good, longer-term |

---

## In brief
Along with cosmetics, natural foods of all types are becoming very

popular. These are foods which do not contain artificial colourings, flavourings and preservatives.

An interesting way to serve this trend is to produce additive-free food by hand at home and supply retail outlets. This would require a food-handling licence, some recipe research, and contacts with cafés, restaurants and food and health shops.

Concentrate exclusively on three or four 'additive-free' food lines, for example, additive-free cakes and pastries, ice cream free of colouring or natural home-baked bread. Arrange a small daily output and supply to suitable outlets on a regular basis.

Catering outlets in themselves are not always enthusiastic about additive-free products. But their customers invariably are and the inclusion of hand-baked 'natural' products would be a considerable sales advantage for them.

Obtain and study books on natural foods and healthy eating. Adapt and cost recipes before you look for possible trade clients to sell your ideas to. Other ideas for outlets, as well as further information on licences etc can be found in **Projects 55** and **57**.

## PROJECT 57: BISCUITS

| | |
|---|---|
| *Status* | Full-time, but could be part-time |
| *Capital required* | Moderate to high |
| *Return* | Long-term |
| *Can be combined with* | Projects 55, 56 and 60 |

### Project facts
There are many opportunities involving food. It's a manufacturing business which is comparatively easy and the profits are notoriously high. One of the most lucrative food businesses today is the making of a very basic product — biscuits.

Over past years the market for 'home-style', rather than factory manufactured biscuits has grown considerably, and this is a sector the entrepreneur can exploit, starting on a very tight budget indeed and growing as business develops.

### What do I need?
● An interest in catering.
● Cash to support product research and launch.
● Suitable premises with equipment. You rent ex-bakery type premises or work from home. Both types will need a food-handling licence from your local Environmental Health De-

partment — and planning consent from the Planning Department.

- The trade journals include *Bakers' Review* and *British Food Journal* (available at main libraries). The trade body is the Federation of Bakers, 20 Bedford Square, London WC1B 3HF.

## Pros and cons

| Pros | Cons |
|------|------|
| Relatively simple to start up | Will take time to get established |
| Good profits can be made | Legal requirements are strict |

## How do I operate?

First comes product development. Biscuits are an expanding market sector and offer hundreds of opportunities within that. First decide what types of biscuit you will make. For the best marketing results you should offer about four different lines. Home-made recipes are invariably best — for example Oatmeal Cookies, Ginger Biscuits, Shortbread Fingers and the like.

Research your products thoroughly. Devise the best ways of making them. In particular, calculate how much one biscuit costs you to produce including all ingredients, baking and labour costs. This is vital for a profitable business.

Obtain supplies of ingredients at best wholesale prices. Look under **Grocery Wholesalers** and **Catering Suppliers** in the Yellow Pages. Establish credit with suppliers for the best cash flow. Engage suitably qualified employees if needed by consulting a recruitment agency or Job Centre.

Arrange suitable packaging. A packaging firm (look under **Boxes — Cardboard** in the Yellow Pages) can advise you. Packaging should always look attractive.

Finally, before going into production, take suitable legal advice from specialist commercial solicitors. This applies especially with regard to price, weight and ingredients, and labelling.

It is best to handle marketing direct. In this way, the 'home-made' nature can be emphasised and the greatest profits made. Approach shops and supermarket groups directly. Offer samples and be prepared to negotiate prices. If necessary, offer your products on a sale-or-return basis to convince them. This technique should always get your product a fair chance.

Gradually, aim to get fixed contracts to supply your products. This allows you to plan production and buying-in well ahead. You can then set production at whatever figure you like and can get orders for 100 biscuits per week or 1,000,000!

You can go on to expand production to cut costs and boost profits, invest in new equipment thus reducing costs, or add new product lines to increase your customer base.

At face value there is nothing special in the manufacture, sale and distribution of biscuits, but, as a business it has many useful characteristics. Most importantly biscuits are a manufactured product (most new businesses nowadays are service based) offering a fairly straightforward start-up without many of the technicalities manufacturing usually involves today. These advantages can be exploited.

## How much can I earn?
**Example:** One small biscuit bakery grew to sales of 800 packets per week within six months. At 40p per packet clear profit (after all expenses paid) this compares favourably as a start-up activity with anything in a similar field.

## Summary
1. You will need a food-handling licence and planning permission to start up. Get legal advice from the start.
2. You will need to research your product thoroughly.
3. Obtain ingredients wholesale.
4. Obtain attractive packaging.
5. Market your product yourself initially.

---

# PROJECT 58: A SANDWICH SERVICE

| | |
|---|---|
| *Status* | Part-time, possibly full-time |
| *Capital required* | Moderate to high |
| *Return* | Very high, medium-term |
| *Can be combined with* | Project 60 |

---

## Project facts
One of the fastest-growing businesses today is food retailing. This applies most of all in the sale of sandwiches and snacks. Good profits are to be had in retailing these, but they can be multiplied by supplying sandwiches on a wholesale basis. This activity is ideal for those with a little culinary ability but it also owes a great deal to imaginative marketing.

## What do I need?

- Possibly a licence.
- Some cash to buy initial ingredients.
- Part-time staff may be necessary.

## Pros and cons

| Pros | Cons |
|------|------|
| Profit margins can be high | May require a licence |
| Easy to run | Will take time to become established |

## How do I operate?

Set up a sandwich production unit. This could be at home or in small, rented 'bakery' type premises. Both may need a licence from your local council. Obtain equipment from catering suppliers.

Do some market research and devise interesting and attractive sandwich recipes. Use the usual ingredients — cheeses, salads, meats etc — but make your sandwiches original in presentation. Make a product range of about 6 – 8 lines. Cost your ingredients and labour for each sandwich so you know the exact cost and use this information to set a price.

Get distributors. Any shops (food or not), petrol stations, cafés, works canteens are possibilities — buying sandwiches 'on contract' is cheaper and easier than making their own. Although some already sell sandwiches from other suppliers they may change for a better commission. Sign agreements, where possible, for a customer to take a number of sandwiches per day (probably Monday – Friday). Then gear your production to supplying that. Get supplies from wholesalers and use part-time staff if necessary. Package attractively. A small van (fitted for food carrying) will be useful for delivering your orders.

There are lots of opportunities for expansion by finding new sales outlets and introducing new lines. Items like pies, crisps, soft drinks, cakes and chocolate bars are all ideal and can be obtained from food wholesalers. Alternatively, or additionally, set up a sandwich shop in small rented premises and retail direct to the public.

## How much can I earn?

Conservative estimates put sandwich and snack gross profit margins at 40% while optimistic estimates approach 120%. So, despite the humble origins, there is certainly potential to develop a substantial business. A small sandwich contract service could well produce 500 pieces weekly (Monday – Friday). At anything between 40p and £1 each, takings and profits can be calculated accordingly.

**Summary**
1. Find out what people want, and devise attractive sandwich recipes to meet that demand.
2. Approach shops, petrol stations, cafés and canteens to sell your sandwiches.
3. Try to get regular orders for a certain number each day, to help with your forward planning.

## PROJECT 59: STREET CATERING

| | |
|---|---|
| *Status* | Mostly part-time, sometimes occasional trade only |
| *Capital required* | Moderate (can be high) |
| *Return* | High, can be fast |

**In brief**
There are many more ways to exploit catering than sandwiches, but some of the most lucrative opportunities remain in snacks, which can be sold on the streets.

Street catering is one of the cheapest forms of retailing, yet one which has high profit margins. You'll need a van, trailer or stand, obtained on outright purchase or lease from a specialist supplier. You'll then need a local authority health certificate and, on some streets, local authority consent to trade. Check with them before starting.

Street stands usually sell snack lines — hot dogs, hamburgers, drinks and (seasonally) ice cream. All are available from wholesale catering suppliers. The business makes a good owner-operated opportunity, but there is potential to employ part-time staff and run a fleet of units.

The main trading advantage is that running costs are so low, usually with no rent to pay, but prices and profit margins can be considerable — up to 150% in some cases. Few shop-based retail methods can compete.

This venture can be run on a 'production line' similar to **Project 58.**

# PROJECT 60: MAKING FOOD FOR RESTAURANTS

| | |
|---|---|
| *Status* | Part-time, possibly full-time |
| *Capital required* | Moderate |
| *Return* | Good, long-term |
| *Can be combined with* | Projects 57, 58, and 59 |

## Project facts

The best products are always made individually and this applies particularly to food. A restaurant offering a wide menu can't hope to make each item individually to order, but to do otherwise is to lose quality. That's why a service hand making, freezing and selling gourmet foods can be so popular. Anyone with a liking for cookery can produce high-quality dishes and sell them on to restaurant outlets. The restaurant can then offer customers both a wide range and good quality!

## What do I need?

- An interest in cooking.
- Possibly a licence.
- Capital for testing and initial ingredients.
- A well-equipped kitchen.
- Recipe books.
- Information can be obtained from the *Food Industry Directory,* the *Frozen and Chilled Foods Year Book* and the trade journal *British Food Journal.*

## Pros and cons

| Pros | Cons |
|---|---|
| Good profits are possible | May need a licence |
| Could be a growth area | Will take time to become established |

## How do I operate?

Use your own kitchen as a base or rent a commercial kitchen. (Check with commercial estate agents.) Both may need a licence from the council's Environmental Health Department. Equip it from a commercial caterers' supplier. Establish links with wholesalers for food items. Look under **Catering Suppliers** and **Grocery Wholesalers** in the Yellow Pages.

Do your market research. Decide on some dishes you can

produce, freeze and sell to restaurants. Check various restaurant menus for suitable items. Products like lasagne, pizzas etc are ideal, but there are more exotic dishes too. Find recipes in cookery books and make them up yourself. After freezing, test them for taste and presentation with your family and friends.

Prepare some sales literature, such as smart typed cards with photographs and descriptions to show customers. Then approach restaurants, pubs, bistros, wine bars etc in the middle range. Be confidential at all times. Some won't be interested publicly, but privately would find it a useful idea. If necessary, offer free samples to try. The best way to sell is by personal call, but you could use a letter — like the one opposite — to make the initial contact.

Secure regular orders to supply certain dishes each week. Gear your production to making them up, freezing and delivering them. (Most items will stay frozen up to one hour in transit.)

You can expand by offering your services to new outlets and introducing new dishes, keeping up quality at all times. The use of a van equipped with a freezer unit allows you to expand into other geographical areas.

**Summary**
1. Do some market research, and decide on the dishes you are going to do.
2. Find suitable recipes and make some dishes to test on family and friends.
3. Prepare sales literature with photographs and descriptions of your dishes.
4. Approach customers, offering free samples if necessary.
5. Try to secure regular orders.

**GOURMET FOODS**
Specialists in Ready Prepared Gourmet Dishes
22 Main Road, Anytown. Tel. 454545.

Dear Sir

Extend Your Menu — With No Extra Work!

I am writing to introduce a brand new gourmet service which allows you to improve even further the service and choice you give to your customers, for virtually no extra work!

Let me explain. Gourmet Foods are experts in the production of quality gourmet food dishes. Using the best of ingredients and authentic natural recipes we're able to create mouthwatering individual dishes from our range of traditional French, Italian or original Polynesian cooking.

All our dishes are made to the same high standards you follow, skilfully cooked then carefully chilled.
And this is where you come in! Our dishes can be offered as extras to your menu. When a customer orders, simply prepare and trim according to our instructions — and serve! Nothing could be simpler. And you have increased customer satisfaction and, ultimately, your reputation.

The service is as simple as it sounds, and is available on an inexpensive, regular basis. So if you would like to know more please give us a call today. We will be delighted to call, with imaginative ideas and samples, and explain just how Gourmet Foods can benefit your business.

Once you've tasted a Gourmet food you'll realise it's not a way of cutting corners. It is simply offering your customers an even better service!

Your sincerely

Gillian Jones

Sample sales letter offering ready-made dishes
to restaurants

# PROJECT 61: BULK BREAKING

| | |
|---|---|
| *Status* | Mainly full-time |
| *Capital required* | Moderate |
| *Return* | Good, long-term |
| *Can be combined with* | Projects 16, 23 and 89 |

## Project facts

Many lucrative businesses thrive on the idea of buying stocks of an item in bulk at low cost, then splitting them into single units for resale at a high unit price. The local supermarket is an example. However, one established success takes this idea right down to the nuts and bolts! Buying bulk hardware (like nuts, bolts and screws) and repacking it into shop-sized packs is just one lucrative sideline in the enormous bulk breaking business.

## What do I need?

- Capital for initial supplies.
- Space for packing.
- Transport.
- Basic business skills.
- *Benn's Hardware and Do-it-Yourself Buyer's Guide* is useful for product ideas, the *Manufacturers and Merchants Directory* will show possible suppliers, and the *Packaging Review Directory* will help in finding packaging supplies.

## Pros and cons

| **Pros** | **Cons** |
|---|---|
| Very easy to run | Will take time to establish |
| A popular service with retailers | |

## How do I operate?

Decide on product lines to handle — check your local hardware shop. Nuts, bolts, nails, screws, pins and hooks are ideal. All are simple products which the public needs in small volume. Then track down manufacturers and distributors (wholesalers are not cheap enough). Cheap supplies can be imported. Buy some small stocks to get you started. Have attractive packaging made. Small plastic bags attached to striking cards and labelled with the contents are ideal. Repack the screws etc into small bags of 12 or

20. Use part-time staff to help. Pack each bag into a box of 50 bags.

Visit local independent hardware shops. Most will want to buy such products, and will surely be interested if you can undercut their present supplier on price or delivery. Sign contracts to take a certain number of packs per month if possible.

You can expand by finding new outlets, adding new products or buying larger bulk to cut prices. Or you can move into other regions, or establish your own brand name.

This way of trading can be expanded to many other popular products, such as sweets, food items, pet supplies and the like. However, hardware is one area where effectiveness has been proved and so it offers a great model.

## How much can I earn?

**Example:** One actual 'bulk repacker' offers almost 50 lines of small hardware items bought in bulk then sold to independent DIY shops. One of their more popular lines is round-head wood screws. These screws are bought for about £1.80 per thousand, then packed into small plastic bags of around 50 each. A box of 20 bags (ie the full thousand) sells to shops for £12. The cost of the bags and packing is about £2 per thousand, so there is ample scope for profit.

## Summary
1. Decide on product lines to handle.
1. Buy from manufacturers and distributors, not wholesalers.
3. Repack into bags of perhaps 12 or 20, and sell in boxes of 50 bags.
4. Sell to local retailers.
5. Try to get a contract for a regular supply.

## PROJECT 62: PICTURE FRAMING

| | |
|---|---|
| *Status* | Part-time, possibly full-time |
| *Capital required* | Low |
| *Return* | Moderate |
| *Can be combined with* | Project 49 |

## Project facts
Some businesses are ideally suited to 'as and when' part-time operation. Picture framing is one of them. It can be established easily, at low cost, yet there are times of brisk demand.

Framing is ideal for those requiring a creative business, possibly from home. The nature of the service is such that a small, personal service can be in considerable demand.

## What do I need?
- A supply of frames and equipment.
- Some basic skill.

## Pros and cons

| Pros | Cons |
| --- | --- |
| Easily established | Needs some skill |
| Demand can be high | Work can be irregular |

## How do I operate?
You will need to stock up with frames and equipment. Several suppliers offer kits, which are advertised in craft magazines. These include ornate frames in many styles, mitre boxes or clamps, saws, pins and glues, plus accessories like stretchers for oils and mounting card for prints.

If you are not already experienced, you will need to practise the skill thoroughly, by framing some sample pictures. Evening classes are available in some areas, and are worth attending.

You can obtain work by various means. You can advertise in the local press for private orders; approach galleries, shops selling prints, photographers, or artists, by letter and offer your service; or approach manufacturers and distributors selling paintings and prints in bulk and negotiate large contracts.

Work on a careful, individual basis. If necessary, employ competent homeworkers to fill bulk orders.

There is nothing really special about picture framing as a business. However, the ability to organise it efficiently and develop it on a large scale basis makes all the difference between a profitable hobby and a lucrative business, yet it can be started from very small beginnings.

## Summary
1. Stock up with supplies and practise the skill.
2. Advertise in the local press for private orders, or approach galleries, shops or distributors for large orders.

# PROJECT 63: REPAIRING AND REFURBISHING

| | |
|---|---|
| *Status* | Part-time/full-time |
| *Capital required* | Moderate |
| *Return* | Good, steady |
| *Can be combined with* | Project 64 |

## Project facts

Few businesses can take junk and turn it into money, but one idea which comes close is the repair and refurbishment of broken or worn household goods.

In times when everyday products are used and then discarded if they break down there is potential to make money repairing them. Frequently such items are worthless in their faulty state, but with a small, inexpensive repair have value as second-hand reconditioned products.

## What do I need?

- Small workshop premises (or you can work at home) and basic tool box.
- Basics skills and interest in electrical and mechanical items.
- A small amount of working capital (£100 upwards).
- The following magazines and journals may give some background information on service/repair: *Do It Yourself, DIY Today, Electrical and Electronic Trader, Mechanical World, Electrical Year Book,* and *Manufacturers and Merchants Directory.*

## Pros and cons

| Pros | Cons |
|---|---|
| Not too much competition in most areas | Special knowledge is an advantage |
| | Profits are limited |

## How do I operate?

The basis of this business is to buy household items which are virtually worthless because of some fault, damage or soiling; then to refurbish them and sell them as good quality, reconditioned products at a much higher price. Some technical knowledge is advisable, but it need only be basic. Many products are suitable: lawn mowers, vacuum cleaners, TV sets, bicycles, motor bikes, washing machines, fridges, cookers and many others.

Buy likely-looking items from auction sales and by advertising in the classified columns of newspapers. Often items that don't work can be bought extremely cheaply, so there is little chance of losing money if they cannot be repaired.

These items should be carefully refurbished. The best way to start is to contact the service department of the manufacturer concerned. In most cases they will be able to suggest ways to cure the fault over the telephone, without the expense of a service engineer.

Reconditioning might involve new parts (use second-hand parts where possible), repairing some damage or just cleaning. Frequently all this can be done very cheaply. If the repair of any item involves a safety hazard (electrical or gas items for example), any work you do should be checked by a qualified person afterwards.

Once the product has been reconditioned it can be resold. This can be done through classified advertisements, or perhaps by selling to second-hand shops for resale. Some repair businesses open a small shop or market stall in order to sell their products.

Although not everybody wants to deal in second-hand products there is undoubtedly a lucrative corner for them. Many car dealers, for example, claim to make more from selling used vehicles than new ones. And this is indicative of the potential that exists in used goods as a whole.

## How much can I earn?

**Example:** One repair business deals in lawnmowers. Broken and neglected machines are bought cheaply in the autumn when no one else will buy them. They are refurbished (mostly just serviced and painted) over the winter and resold in the spring.

A typical five-year-old petrol-engined mower of a good quality brand could be bought for £80, in need of repair. With careful painting, service and parts costing a total of £25 this firm would sell the self-same mower in March or April for £195!

## Summary
1. Buy faulty, damaged or soiled household items cheaply at auctions and by advertising.
2. Refurbish them, with help from the manufacturer's service department if necessary.
3. If there is likely to be any safety risk, such as with electrical or gas appliances, get the work checked by a qualified person.

# PROJECT FILE 64: SECOND-HAND FURNITURE

| | |
|---|---|
| *Status* | Part-time/full-time |
| *Capital required* | Low |
| *Return* | Moderate to good |
| *Can be combined with* | Projects 6 and 63 |

## Project facts

There is ample potential for sales in the 'used' market and this is ideal for exploitation in a low-capital business. Cars are the typical 'used' business but there is scope to extend it into furniture. A used furniture business can be started easily, and dealing in used furniture does not necessarily involve you in antiques, nor need any specialist knowledge.

## What do I need?

- Some capital for initial purchases.
- Storage and display space (nothing too elaborate).
- A van.

## Pros and cons

| Pros | Cons |
|---|---|
| Can be bought cheaply and sold at a good profit when 'done up' | Needs storage space. You could be left with unsold goods |

## How do I operate?

Start by obtaining stock. Visit all the local furniture and household effects auctions regularly. Use whatever capital you have to buy up anything on offer that is sound but cheap. This will range from some quite valuable pieces to 'junk'. As long as you pay rock-bottom prices you don't need an expert eye — anything will do.

Transport your 'finds' to a place of storage — either a small lock-up unit or a garage. It's a good idea to make contact with an antique furniture dealer who will call on you now and then. Occasionally, valuable pieces can be spotted!

The main aim of your business, however, is to refurbish items of furniture for resale. For this you can establish a small workshop at home or in premises. Frequently items which are almost valueless can be cleaned and repainted, serviced or repaired to make quite well-priced, presentable second-hand goods.

There are two principal groups of used furniture buyers. First, those who can't afford new items. Secondly (and quite a large group) those who don't *want* new furniture — for example, to furnish rented accommodation or a holiday cottage. Sell to both — prices are generally much higher than you would expect. Perfect furniture is not expected, but it must be clean.

Try to get some sort of 'workshop showroom' to display your goods in. (You could rent one.) Also advertise in the local press and with shop window cards. Most newspapers have classified columns where items of £100 – £150 will sell readily. Be flexible on prices and take furniture 'part exchanges' if asked — they can be used as new stock.

Dealing in just a few items per week can make an excellent sideline business, but there is scope to expand. For example, you can operate on a wholesale basis supplying (or even setting up) a number of used furniture shops. You could eventually move to genuine antiques — but this is not necessary when starting up.

## How much can I earn?

A major new sector of this business involves used upholstery. For example, one dealer buys three-piece suites from auctions for £5 – £10. These are steam cleaned (by a contractor for £20), tidied and resold for £90 – £100. Another dealer specialises in buying and stripping painted wood furniture and then hand-finishing to a high standard. His pieces aren't antiques but make a great substitute for those who like, but can't afford, genuine antique furniture.

## Summary

1. Buy furniture from auctions, making sure it is sound.
2. Store it and refurbish it where necessary.
3. Advertise in the press, and have a showroom where people can see the furniture.

---

## PROJECT 65: REUPHOLSTERY

| | |
|---|---|
| *Status* | Part-time/full-time |
| *Capital required* | Moderate |
| *Return* | Moderate to high |
| *Can be combined with* | Projects 63 and 64 |

---

### Project facts

Hand craft services are always popular and a rather special one is upholstery. Modern upholstered furniture is very keenly priced and hence not always covered in the most durable fabric. When it becomes worn the only alternative to complete replacement is reupholstery.

Upholstery is an old craft and quite rare nowadays, yet with basic skills it is not too difficult to do. So it makes a good 'starter' business, initially part-time, moving to full-time later.

## What do I need?
- Space to work.
- Specialist tools.
- A van.
- Some degree of skill.
- Periodicals like *Drapers Record, Embroidery, Textile Horizons* and *Textile Month* and the *British Textile Register,* an annual guide, will provide background information.

## Pros and cons

**Pros**

Very healthy demand
Allows you to learn a
  valuable handicraft.

**Cons**

Needs time to learn and
  develop basic skills
Needs time to establish a
  good reputation

## How do I operate?
Reupholstery work needs space. A dry, heated garage could be used, or a small workshop unit. You can really only operate locally at first. Advertise in the local press or on shop window cards. There is good repeat and recommendation trade for a good service. Three-piece suites are the most popular and most profitable items. Handle individual upholstered chairs as 'fillers' only.

A degree of skill is required. For inexpensive training look to evening classes. Some specialist tools are needed, such as buttonhooks and upholsterers' needles, and you can get them from upholsterers' suppliers in most major towns. Look under **Upholsterers' Suppliers** in the Yellow Pages.

You need a selection of fabrics. Consult textile wholesalers. Many will loan you pattern books which customers can choose from. Fabrics can then be bought as needed with no need for stocks. Cotton prints and synthetic velvet (of which Dralon is the leading brand) are the most popular lines.

When you are ready, you can invite enquiries for your work.

Give estimates free and aim to offer a high quality service for a high price. This is generally better than a budget service. The usual procedure is to handle one three-piece suite within the week — a free loan suite while you do the work is a good sales point!

Techniques for reupholstery vary. The golden rule is that new fabric should be put on in exactly the same form as the old. One method is therefore to unpick all the old fabric sections and use these as patterns to cut new fabric, and then to restitch or tack them into place in exactly the same way. With this technique there is room for some minor modification to items of trim, but you must adhere to the old style as much as possible. In most cases the original manufacturer will have designed the frame specifically for that sort of upholstery, and no other.

Finish off to a high standard and return the furniture to your customer. A three- or six-month guarantee on materials and workmanship is another good sales point.

A part-time business can handle one suite per week, expanding as required. Once established, contact furniture stores. They could offer customers a reupholstery service which you carry out for them for, say, a 20% commission. Your business could expand regionally with such organisation.

## Summary
1. Operate locally at first. Advertise in the local press and in shop windows.
2. Attend evening classes if you do not already have the skill.
3. Try to obtain pattern books from wholesalers to avoid having to carry too much stock.
4. Give free estimates, and aim to provide a good quality service at a high price.

## PROJECT 66: CONTRACT MAINTENANCE

| | |
|---|---|
| *Status* | Part-time/full-time |
| *Capital required* | Low |
| *Return* | Moderate |
| *Can be combined with* | Projects 27, 67 and 68 |

### Project facts
So many business opportunities exist because companies can't afford to employ staff to do seemingly unimportant jobs. A prime example of this is contract maintenance. There are thousands of

businesses with premises, where maintenance is nobody's actual job, and so there is scope to offer a service doing, or just arranging, those odd jobs.

## What do I need?
- A van.
- Basic cleaning and gardening equipment.
- Part-time employees if necessary.

## Pros and cons

| Pros | Cons |
|---|---|
| Very little investment needed | Only a moderate income can be expected |
| Can expand quite rapidly | Will take time for business to build up |

## How do I operate?
Advertise your contract maintenance service in the local press, or write to or call on possible business customers. Virtually anyone with a shop, office, or small factory could be a potential customer. An example of a letter promoting such a service is given on the next page.

Call personally on those who are interested, and find out their regular maintenance requirements. This could be window cleaning, gardening, car park sweeping, dustbin emptying or any similar work. You will be offering to do small, easy jobs which are not sufficient for a full-time employee.

Agree a fee for attending to these matters weekly or bi-weekly. Make a simple written agreement, and have the fee paid to you by direct debit to your bank account.

Next, advertise for part-time employees through Job Centres. Provide them with a van (which you could buy second-hand or lease), overalls and basic gardening and cleaning tools. They go out and do the job, while you supervise them to ensure the customer is satisfied. But you should spend most of your time finding new customers, increasing the workforce as necessary.

There is nothing really complex about such a service, but the way it is organised makes it profitable. You might, for example, charge a small office £15 weekly for cleaning windows, sweeping up outside, tidying the garden area etc — quite reasonable for the work involved. Although it is not a lot in itself it adds up over 52 weeks (780) and over 50 similar concerns (£39,000)! Your labour costs might only be £2 or so per hour, giving ample scope for profit.

## ABC MAINTENANCE
23 The Road, Anytown. Tel. 567567.

Dear Sirs,

### WE'LL DO ANYTHING YOU DON'T WANT TO!

Amazing, isn't it, all those little jobs that crop up around your shop or office? But they aren't really your job — and no one ever wants to do them! There are things like small repairs and general maintenance, window cleaning, gardening, cleaning, occasional painting, small removals, sweeping up, rubbish disposal — even changing the light bulbs!

Now, however, there is a brand new service designed to do the jobs that no one else wants to do. We'll undertake those jobs quickly, competently and with the minimum of supervision, all on a regular basis for a small regular fee. It sounds useful doesn't it? And it'll save you work, and keep your premises up to scratch.

If this sounds like the sort of service you could use why not give us a ring today? We'll tell you how easily we can handle it and how little it could cost.

After all, your time should be spent running your business, not doing things you don't want to do.

Yours faithfully


P. Griffiths

Sample letter offering a contract maintenance service

The contract element makes otherwise unprofitable work rather lucrative. It is a principle which can be applied to many other business ideas.

## Summary

1. Advertise your service in the press, or write to or visit potential customers.
2. Aim at businesses which are not big enough to have a maintenance department of their own.
3. Make a written agreement, and have payments made by direct debit to your bank.
4. Supervise the work to ensure that the customer is satisfied.

---

# PROJECT 67: EQUIPMENT CLEANING

| | |
|---|---|
| *Status* | Part-time/full-time |
| *Capital required* | Very low |
| *Return* | Good, regular |
| *Can be combined with* | Project 66 |

---

## Project facts

Nowadays electronic equipment is commonplace in any office or shop and much of it is quite expensive and sophisticated. This means it has to be carefully looked after, but few companies are properly equipped to do this. Regular cleaning is an important job, but incorrectly done the results can be disastrous! Warranties for most types of equipment — telephones, computers, photocopiers — are invalidated if they are cleaned in the wrong way.

This problem gives scope for a small but lucrative service, offering high-tech cleaning to businesses with large amounts of equipment. The demand for such a service is sure to grow in the future!

## What do I need?

- Part-time staff.
- The ability to sell a new service.

## Pros and cons

| Pros | Cons |
|---|---|
| Can provide a regular income | May take time for the idea to become established |
| No specialist knowledge is needed | |

## How do I operate?

Promote your service by writing to business users of large amounts of electronic equipment. Better still, engage a sales representative (advertise for one in the press) to visit firms in the region. Pay him on commission. Such a service operates best on contract. The customer pays a set amount monthly by direct debit to your bank. Set your fee according to the amount of work involved.

No specialist knowledge is needed to sell the service but when you sign up customers visit them to see what equipment they have. This will range from telephone equipment to computers, photocopiers, facsimile machines, typewriters, calculators and much else. Make a note of the manufacturers. Next, contact these companies and seek their guidance on correct cleaning. Take note of the materials, chemicals and procedures they recommend for cleaning the equipment without risk of damage. Write up a short 'cleaning bulletin' for the various items.

Staff for such an operation can be engaged through Job Centres. They should be careful and thoughtful. Part-time evening workers are ideal. Supply them with cleaning materials (look under **Janitorial Supplies** in the Yellow Pages for suppliers) and brief them on cleaning procedures.

Finally, supervise the staff cleaning the equipment. As long as it operates competently each contract brings you a regular income. The customer benefits from a smart office, correctly functioning equipment and preservation of any valuable warranty that exists.

## How much can I earn?

No current exclusive operators of this service are known, but one small company offers a 'phone cleanse' service, disinfecting office telephones as an add-on to contract cleaning. It has 45 local customers for the service, each paying an average of £3 per week. The work is done by a part-timer working three hours each evening (Monday – Friday) and paid £2.80 per hour.

## Summary

1. Promote the service yourself or hire a sales representative.
2. Get a contract, with payment by direct debit to your bank.
3. Establish what equipment the customer has, and contact the manufacturers to find out the recommended cleaning materials and method.
4. Hire careful part-time cleaners to do the work under your supervision.

# PROJECT 68: A LAUNDRY SERVICE

| | |
|---|---|
| *Status* | Part-time, later full-time |
| *Capital required* | Very low |
| *Return* | Steady |
| *Can be combined with* | Projects 66 and 67 |

## Project facts

Cleaning services generally make healthy businesses. However, it is usually better to find a lucrative new cleaning idea rather than try to compete with existing services head-on.

Commercial laundries tend to handle only large items, while domestic laundry services are now quite rare. Yet there is a demand for laundry facilities for small- and medium-sized companies. The laundering of the towels in the lavatories and the curtains in reception is 'no one's job' in a small firm, and a new laundry service can fill that need.

## What do I need?

- Space — a spare room or garage is ideal. Later you could rent a workshop unit.
- Washing, drying and ironing facilities. Buy a washing machine, drier, irons etc second-hand if necessary.
- Transport.

## Pros and cons

| Pros | Cons |
|---|---|
| Needs virtually no investment | Income is steady but low |

## How do I operate?

The selling of the service is important. You are aiming at all small- and medium-sized businesses who probably don't have existing contractors. Use the Yellow Pages as a source of small business leads, following up those who appear interested with a personal visit.

The aim of your service is not to compete with the cleansing of workwear and similar items, but to offer a service for small items, such as kitchen and washroom towels, tea-towels, curtains, cushion covers and the like. Priced at a modest level most smaller concerns would find this service useful.

Sign interested customers up on a contract basis, so that they pay a monthly amount for you to launder everything as necessary. There is little profit in 'one-off' laundry jobs. Similarly you will need a large number of customers to achieve satisfactory profits — 40 or 50 would be ideal.

Because individual charges can never be very high you need to organise an efficient service for collecting, washing and returning items. Check that the customer has a double supply of everything. Then one week, you collect items for cleaning. Over the next week, wash, dry and iron them. Keep a careful watch on costs, such as electricity, cleansing materials, and labour. In the second week, return clean items to the customer, and collect the next batch of dirty items for cleaning. Obtain payment monthly by direct debit to your bank account.

Items cleaned infrequently, like curtains, will need to be cleaned and returned within two or three days at most and extra charges need to be applied for the extra labour and transport costs involved. This sort of service can significantly boost the moderate regular takings.

For maximum profit, offer extra services like the supply of new linen, mending and repair, alterations, dry cleaning or carpet and upholstery cleaning. To start without capital investment you could simply sell these services and ask a competent subcontractor to do the work for you.

## How much can I earn?

In this business profits are very closely connected to sales effort. It is best to aim for a large number of customers who all use the service on a regular contract basis.

**Example:** One established laundry handles around 5,000 pieces per week at an average 50p item charge. A new service would ideally need to aim for at least 40 to 50 local customers all paying at least £10 a week. Expenses in running such a service should work out at about 25% of takings.

## Summary
1. The selling of the service is all-important.
2. Sign customers up on a regular contract basis, with monthly payments by direct debit.
3. Organise an efficient 'round' of collection, washing and returning items.
4. To increase your profits, you can offer extra services like mending and alterations.

# PROJECT 69: CAR VALETING

| | |
|---|---|
| *Status* | Mostly full-time |
| *Capital required* | Moderate to high |
| *Return* | Good |
| *Can be combined with* | Projects 67 and 68 |

## Project facts
There are a number of opportunities for providing a cleaning service, but there is one that is especially noteworthy — car valeting. It is an attractive proposition because of the enormous potential demand, ease of operation and regularity of use by customers.

The best way to start in car valeting is at the top of the trade, offering a volume service and getting contract work. This can be achieved far more easily and for a far smaller investment than many comparable cleaning activities.

## What do I need?
- Premises capable of taking several cars.
- Equipment.
- Part-time or full-time staff.

## Pros and cons

| Pros | Cons |
|---|---|
| Volume contracts are not difficult to get | Needs quite a lot of capital |
| No special skill is required | Competition could be strong |

## How do I operate?
Obtain premises and equipment. A small workshop unit, capable of taking about six cars under cover, or a small garage, would be ideal. A hot water pressure washer for exteriors and carpet steam cleaner for interiors are the only major items of equipment you need. There are specialist suppliers, and machines can be leased. Cleaning materials, polishes etc can be obtained from the same suppliers. Look under **Cleaning Materials Manufacturers and Suppliers** in the Yellow Pages.

Part- or full-time unskilled staff can be employed, and can easily be trained in cleaning techniques. You will also need a competent receptionist to answer customer enquiries and organise bookings.

Advertise your service in the local press and the Yellow Pages to get custom from the public, but also canvass trade customers. These include new and used car dealers, car hire firms, taxi firms, car auctions and fleet operators. Sell the service to these businesses in person, perhaps engaging a freelance sales representative. Some trade customers already have trade contracts, but will be tempted by a better deal.

Offer different levels of service, such as the whole car or exterior only. Wash, polish and clean the exterior and interior as necessary to a high standard.

You can expand with more regular contracts, more space and more staff, and also offer coach, lorry, van, motorcycle and caravan cleaning.

## How much can I earn?
**Example:** One car valet service has contracts with four local franchised car dealers to prepare all their new and used vehicles. They handle about 38 vehicles weekly at £22 each, and 20 vehicles at £30. They also clean another twelve vehicles direct from the public at £30 – £40 each for a thorough interior and exterior clean. Total weekly takings are about £1,850. There is certainly scope to increase this volume several times over in time.

## Summary
1.  You will need premises to work from, and special cleaning equipment.
2.  Aim for contract work, offering a volume service to trade customers.
3.  Advertise to the public in the local press, but canvass trade customers personally.
4.  Offer different levels of service to suit the customer's requirements.
5.  A high level of service will allow you to charge high prices and bring the repeat business on which this venture depends.

# PROJECT 70: ALARM INSTALLATION

| | |
|---|---|
| *Status* | Full-time, could be part-time |
| *Capital required* | Moderate |
| *Return* | Good, short-term |
| *Can be combined with* | Projects 5, 51, 52 and 53 |

## Project facts

The prevention of burglary and vandalism has become big business, with many different products and services available to combat the threat. Of these, one of the fastest growing is the supply and fitting of intruder alarms. Demand is now considerable and growing as alarms descend the social scale. In business terms this means that alarms are often considered essential even on quite ordinary properties.

Modern electronic developments in alarms have greatly simplified planning and installation, right down to basic electrics level. Combine this with imaginative selling and you have a business that is not only modern but growing.

## What do I need?

- Good persuasive skills.
- Basic electrical knowledge.
- A small amount of capital for advertising and stock.
- Transport.
- The professional association is the National Supervisory Council for Intruder Alarms (NSCIA), though it is not necessary to be a member of any trade organisation to start up.

## Pros and cons

| Pros | Cons |
|---|---|
| This is a growth area | Needs some basic knowledge |
| Easy to set up | Needs selling skills |

## How do I operate?

One advantage of this business is that you can start to sell virtually from day one. There will be many local sources of business. Homes in the middle income range are the best bet initially, rather than the more difficult commercial alarms.

Widespread advertising is necessary to start. Use all the usual methods — press, leaflets, door-to-door calling and perhaps demonstration stands in supermarkets. It can be a good idea to employ part-time sales canvassers on commission. From these leads a more personal approach should be used. This can be a good job for the owner-operator (or a sales representative). Home visits are usually offered and styled as a 'Free Security Survey and Alarm Quote'.

Many alarm component suppliers offer a free design service. You simply send them a sketch of your customer's property, and they design an alarm and quote for supplying the parts. Onto this, you just add labour costs and a profit element of 50% – 100%.

This is a business where cheapest is not always regarded as best, so the business that portrays a professional image can often charge the very highest prices, around £600 – £800 for installing a system in a medium-sized three bedroomed detached house. Few people enquire about an alarm out of interest. They are usually serious. So careful negotiation involving the price and presentation can clinch the deal in a high percentage of cases. A 50% – 70% conversion rate would be quite realistic.

There are many alarm component suppliers. To locate some look in a journal like *Exchange & Mart*. They will design a system and supply every part needed as a complete kit.

It is not necessary to know much about alarms at the start. Most centre round an electronic control box. This is wired to detectors at possible points of entry in the home. The alarm is raised by an outside bell or siren. Most systems are essentially the same technically.

This can be a good owner-operated business for someone with basic DIY skills, but it is also suitable for taking on semi-skilled employees, using basic tools. Most systems work on a low voltage, not directly wired into mains electricity, so no electrical qualifications are required.

Alarm component suppliers will supply fitting instructions for parts, and many operate a telephone 'hotline' to help with installation. Basically the work centres around laying discreet cable runs, drilling holes and mounting connectors. Ask the supplier for a system to British Standard 4737. This is evidence of the quality of the system for the customer.

Lucrative sidelines to offer are a breakdown service and annual maintenance inspection, possibly at a set fee plus parts. Each year you call to service the alarm. Such repairs are usually quite inexpensive and straightforward — little repair knowledge as such is needed, but they build a regular income.

The whole idea behind security alarm supply is that it is much less complex than it looks. Hence an entrepreneur who knows where to get his information can start with very little more than a basic knowledge. You can start on a very simple basis, perhaps by fitting your own home alarm.

## How much can I earn?

A costing for an alarm system for a typical 3 bedroomed semi-detached home might be:

| | |
|---|---:|
| Parts and components, from wholesalers   approx | £120 |
| Cost of advertising to get that one order, and cost of completing survey etc.   approx | £80 |
| Labour costs, 1–2 days work   approx | £65 |
| Sundry expenses (travel etc)   approx | £35 |
| TOTAL | £300 |
| Add typical profit margin of 100%   approx | £300 |
| Hence, typical selling price of alarm   approx | £600 |

## Summary
1.  Aim for middle-income homes initially.
2.  Advertise in the press, leaflets, door-to-door calling and possibly a demonstration stand.
3.  Visit the client personally, and draw a sketch of the property.
4.  The alarm component supplier will design a system and supply the parts which you instal.
5.  Most people who enquire are serious, so you should be able to sign up a high percentage of initial enquirers.

# Creative and Artistic Businesses

These projects are ideal for people who have some creative or artistic talents. Some are concerned with making things, others just involve ideas. But they all offer scope for imaginative flair.

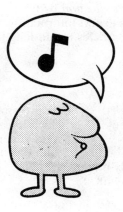

# PROJECT 71: WRITING ABOUT YOUR INTERESTS

| | |
|---|---|
| *Status* | Part-time, occasional |
| *Capital required* | Moderate |
| *Return* | Good, fast |
| *Can be combined with* | Projects 24, 72 and 73 |

## Project facts

Everyone has a story in them, and it needn't be as complicated as you think to get it out. Other people could well want to know about your skills or experiences. You don't have to write a novel to profit from them.

If you have some sort of skill or hobby you could write it up as a non-fiction book, then publish it yourself and sell it to other enthusiasts. It has been done before and means you don't need a publisher to make money from your own book.

Are you interested in angling? That could be the basis for a book. So could photography, plumbing, driving or holidaymaking!

## What do I need?

- The idea for a book.
- An ability to write clearly and concisely.
- A typewriter is desirable.
- The *Writers' and Artists' Yearbook,* available in main libraries and bookshops, will provide useful contacts.
- *British Books in Print,* available at main libraries, will help you find out what competing books there are.
- *How to Write for Publication* by Chriss McCallum (Northcote House, 1989) gives expert information and advice on all types of writing — from articles to full-length books — and how to get published.

## Pros and cons

| Pros | Cons |
|---|---|
| Investment can be phased and is not all required at once | Some investment is needed which is lost if project fails |
| Once established, satisfied customers will readily buy further books you might produce | Success depends on whether potential customers take to the idea |

178

## How do I operate?

First, decide your subject. It should be something you know quite well, but you don't need to be an authority. Then decide on a provisional title. This may not be the final title but you must have something to keep in mind. Decide the length — 15,000 words is ideal.

Write a plan to show what you will write about chapter by chapter. If you find it helps, note down every *paragraph* you will write. Then write your book according to the plan. Type it if possible but longhand will be all right if you cannot type. Refine it by rewriting and rewriting until it reads 'just right'.

When your writing is complete have the book typed professionally, even if you have typed it yourself already. Then take it to a booklet printer. (Look under **Printers** in the Yellow Pages.) Get three quotes before deciding which printer to use. An A5 sized paperback is about right. 500 or 1,000 copies will usually be enough.

The next step is selling. The best way to do this initially is by mail order in enthusiast magazines and journals. Identify suitable ones through *Benn's Media Directory*. For example, a book called *How to Buy a New Car at a Discount* might sell well in *What Car?* Write a classified ad and place it in a suitable magazine. Try several magazines and ads over several different months, and repeat your ad in those which bring the best response. As the orders come in take cheques and post out the copies of your book.

You can expand by writing new books on the same subject or books on other subjects. Or you can refine your mail order selling techniques, or offer the book to an existing publisher for publication as a 'bookshop book'. They may be especially interested if the book has a proven sales record in the small mail order market.

## How much can I earn?

**Example:** Consider these actual figures for the publication of a small manual on business ideas, self published and sold by mail order. It was printed by a local printer from a typed manuscript and then sold by advertisements in a single business magazine:

| | |
|---|---|
| Costs of research, writing, typing and production of manuscript | £80.00 |
| Printing of 500 copies in paperback form and delivery to publisher | £302.00 |

| | |
|---|---|
| 20 classified advertisements in magazine at £11.50 each, total cost | £230.00 |
| Printed sales leaflets used to send out to customers who enquired from advertisements, total cost | £65.00 |
| 450 copies sold in 3 months: cost of posting these orders to customers | £99.00 |
| TOTAL COSTS & EXPENSES | £776.00 |
| 450 copies sold at £11 per copy (typical price for this sort of book): | |
| TOTAL SALES VALUE | £4,950.00 |

So, total profit from this project (excluding some sundry expenses) would be in the region of £4,000 plus.

## Summary

1. Decide on a subject you know something about, and then decide on a provisional title for your book.
2. Write a plan, chapter by chapter, or even paragraph by paragraph, and follow that plan as you write.
3. Type it if you can, but otherwise write it in longhand.
4. Have it professionally typed, and get it printed by a booklet printer — get at least three quotes from printers.
5. Sell it by means of classified ads in specialist magazines.

---

## PROJECT 72: TRAVEL WRITING

| | |
|---|---|
| *Status* | Part-time, occasional |
| *Capital required* | Low |
| *Return* | High, but can be irregular |
| *Can be combined with* | Project 42 |

---

## Project facts

There are many opportunities in writing, but it is difficult to find one that is as exciting as well as offering enjoyable rewards, as travel writing.

With travel writing there are opportunities both to travel, often free, internationally and to be paid for your work. There is a healthy demand for travel books.

## What do I need?

- The ability to write clearly and concisely.
- A typewriter and the ability to use it would be useful.

- The *Writers' and Artists' Yearbook* gives details of publishers and their interests.
- Existing travel books will give you ideas on approach and content.
- The professional association is the British Guild of Travel Writers, 31 Riverside Court, Caversham, Reading, Berkshire RG4 8AL (Tel. (0743) 481384).

## Pros and cons

| Pros | Cons |
|------|------|
| You could get free travel as well as being paid for your work | You may put in a lot of work and not find a publisher |

## How do I operate

Decide where you want to visit and where you want to write about. A tourist area of the UK is a good starter, before branching out to Europe and then other continents. Consult existing travel guides to give you ideas — the 'Fodors' series is one of the most comprehensive.

Write a synopsis of your book or booklet including a list of all chapters, sections, appendices and subjects to be covered. Write about twenty double-spaced pages of the book as a sample. Use (but do not copy) existing travel books as a guide. Identify publishers who publish similar travel books, and send them all a copy of your proposals with a covering letter explaining your idea. Keep up this canvassing of publishers until you find one who will offer to publish the book you intend to write on royalty terms. If you receive no offers after six attempts then try another subject.

Once you have found a publisher, sign an author's agreement with them — they will usually provide a form for this. Then, contact embassies, tourist offices, tour operators, airlines and hoteliers who operate in the area in question. Explain that you are writing a book and ask if they will provide free or subsidised facilities for your research trip.

The response to such requests will vary. Some may be unco-operative, but it is not unusual for an airline to provide a free or reduced-price flight, hotels to provide free accommodation and tourist offices to offer a free hire car or admission to places of interest. Your trip may not be completely free, but you could well have only modest, minor expenses. Ideally, get your publisher to give you a letter confirming the publishing deal. It will carry great weight with airlines, hotels etc.

Undertake your trip and gather all the information you need. Collect existing books and brochures on the area. Take photographs and notes while you are there. When you return home, write your book according to the established synopsis, filling in the details from the material you have gathered. If writing is not your strong point record your book on audio tape and get a professional writer to write it up for you.

Submit the completed manuscript to the publisher. They will publish and pay royalties as per your agreement. If the book does especially well you may be able to offer them a series of similar books. Such a success will also get you more free facilities on your next trip.

### How much can I earn?
More than one writer draws an annual royalty cheque of about £5,000 for such a book, and they often have sufficient requests for their service to undertake research for three or four further books each year if they want to.

### Summary
1. Decide where you want to visit — it is best to start in the UK.
2. Consult existing guides, and write a synopsis of your book.
3. Submit this to a number of publishers.
4. If a publisher accepts your proposal, contact tourist offices, tour operators and hotels, to see if they are prepared to subsidise your trip.
5. Read existing books on the area, make your own notes and take photographs while you are there.
6. Write the book on your return, from your notes and other information.

## PROJECT 73: WRITING VERSE FOR GREETINGS CARDS

| | |
|---|---|
| *Status* | Part-time only |
| *Capital required* | Very little |
| *Return* | Moderate to low |

### Project facts
There are openings in many forms of writing, but few where money is made for such brief pieces as in poetry. Within this, the writing of verse for greetings cards offers a ready market.

This sort of opportunity is more for the creative and imaginative person, with some liking and perhaps experience in writing their own verse. It may never be one of the bigger earners, but it does offer the chance of good sideline income, plus more satisfaction than most opportunities.

## What do I need?
- The ability to write good verse to order.
- The *Writers' and Artists' Yearbook* will have details of card publishers.
- The Poetry Society, 21 Earls Court Square, London SW5 9DE and the Society of Authors, 84 Drayton Gardens, London SW10 9SB (Tel. 01-373 6642) might be of some help.
- Most verse buyers are members of the Greetings Card and Calender Association.
- *Poetry Nation*, *Poetry Now* and *Poetry Review* are magazines which might give ideas and techniques.

## Pros and cons
**Pros**

Makes a pleasant sideline

**Cons**

Income is low and irregular.

## How do I operate?
Research the market thoroughly. Collect greetings cards of all types — birthday and Christmas cards are more usual, but there are now cards for everything from leaving a job to moving into a new house. Assemble your own folder of examples. Study the examples carefully. Note the sort of language used, the style, the length and the subjects. Try writing your own verse which fits in with those patterns, but on original subjects. Keep another file of your best creations.

Finally, check the possible markets for your work — principally card manufacturers and publishers. You will find details in press directories, also in the *Writers' and Artists' Yearbook*. Find examples of these firms' cards and study their requirements.

When you are well informed on the market for verse you can start to market your services. Do this by writing to a number of card publishers. Emphasise your thoughtfulness and originality, but send no samples. A few companies use only in-house verse. But the vast majority will at least consider submissions. When they reply send them some further information about yourself, plus a neatly presented folder of samples of your verse.

As with any freelance writing, be prepared for rejections, but there is an excellent chance that several companies will be interested in retaining you as a part-time verse writer. If so, proceed on a job-by-job basis. The company will explain the type of verse they require for a new card they are publishing. You negotiate the price, then write perhaps two or three alternatives, one of which should fit the bill exactly! If the verse succeeds on the first card there is every chance you will be commissioned time after time.

## How much can I earn?
One semi-professional verse writer is employed by a small greetings card publisher for twenty hours per month. Their rate of pay is £8 per hour and could be much more. Another verse writer sells his work on an unsolicited basis and expects to sell two or three items per month at £40 – £60 each.

## Summary
1.  Research the market thoroughly before you start.
2.  Write to card publishers offering your services, and send samples of your work to those who respond.
3   You will be told what sort of verse the company needs for a particular card, and you should submit two or three alternatives. You will be paid if they accept one of them.

---

## PROJECT 74: CALLIGRAPHY

| | |
|---|---|
| *Status* | Part-time only |
| *Capital required* | Very low |
| *Return* | Good, long-term |
| *Can be combined with* | Projects 62 and 89 |

---

## Project Facts
Calligraphy is the practice of writing, in particular, classic handwriting styles of the past. Although it has been an academic subject, it now offers potential as a business. Fine calligraphic script is highly regarded and desirable in producing a wide range of items from menus in exclusive restaurants to high-class wedding invitations.

A steady hand and eye for detail are the only basic requirements. No investment or experience is necessary. Although calligraphy can never be big business it does hold sufficient potential for a lucrative owner-operated sideline.

## What do I need?
- Skills in calligraphy.
- A calligraphy pen and a selection of nibs.
- Back issues of art journals or magazines may have articles on calligraphy.
- Historical societies may be able to help with research into styles for more advanced jobs. The Royal Historical Society, Gower Street, London WC1E 6BT could provide contacts.

## Pros and cons

| Pros | Cons |
|---|---|
| No investment needed | Needs some skill and creative ability |
| Can become quite lucrative | Will take time to build up |

## How do I operate?
Initially, you need to learn the skills of calligraphy, both as regards penmanship and the different calligraphic styles. You will need to take lessons — there are evening classes in many areas. An alternative is to consult books on the subject, but classes are better.

The only equipment you need is a pen with a selection of different nibs. Inexpensive calligraphy sets are available at stationers. Good quality bond paper is sufficient for practice.

Experiment and rehearse the various skills so that you can write any document in calligraphic lettering. The styles you should learn (covered in most calligraphy books) are Gothic (or Black Letter), Italic, Copperplate, Roman and Uncial. Any others are optional.

Having acquired the basic skills, you can turn to offering your services in producing skilfully written documents for many purposes. A regular ad in local newspapers will bring enquiries, but do be prepared to wait for your name to get known. Charge for your work by the hour — at least £20 or so.

Attractive calligraphic documents have great appeal, and although not everybody can afford them some exclusive uses are:

- producing 'originals' for printers
- menus for exclusive restaurants
- notices for hotels
- invitations for exclusive parties, weddings etc
- shop window display cards
- certificates for schools and colleges

- important official documents for the public and business customers (for example, solicitors)

You may be able to think up other uses. Calligraphy is an individual skill — and ideal for those who want to gain satisfaction from a business activity.

## Summary
1. If you do not already know how to do calligraphy, you will have to learn — preferably at evening classes.
2. Experiment and practise with various styles and designs.
3. Place a regular advertisement in the local paper. You may have to wait for your name to become known.
4. Charge by the hour.

---

## PROJECT 75: VIDEO FILM PRODUCTION

| | |
|---|---|
| *Status* | Part-time, full time |
| *Capital required* | Moderate to high |
| *Return* | High, short-term |
| *Can be combined with* | Projects 76 and 77 |

---

### Project facts
The advent of hand-held video cameras has given rise to many business opportunities. With a video camera you have the capability to produce a wide variety of valuable and versatile video films.

### What do I need?
- A video camera, monitor, lighting and recording equipment — these can be hired initially, and bought later.
- Some skill in using the equipment.
- The trade journals *Video Week* and *Television,* and the amateur magazine *Amateur Video* will give ideas and advice, and are available at main libraries.

### Pros and cons
| Pros | Cons |
|---|---|
| Demand is growing quickly | Competition is increasing |
| There are many new uses for video presentations | Capital investment could be high for anything more than a small business |

## How do I operate?

Contact an equipment hire firm in one of the major centres for the equipment you need. You will need some skill in operating it if you are to do so professionally, so if you have had no previous experience you should spend some time practising to ensure that your results are of a sufficiently high standard, or preferably attend a course.

Once you are satisfied that you have the skill, you can start advertising your services through the local or specialist press, leaflets and direct mail. The actual methods used will depend on what services you are offering, but all will have to be heavily promoted. Here are a few ideas:

1.  Weddings. A well-established and successful service exists in recording weddings. You could do more with imaginative selling.
2.  Graduations. A newer service offering a video record of university and college graduation ceremonies has room for exploitation. Sell the idea to colleges. They could make it known to students for you and you pay them a commission.
3.  Training Films, for companies to use in staff training schemes.
4.  Sales Productions. A sort of 'video brochure' of a particular product to assist in selling it, especially by mail order. For example, some companies selling DIY products produce a video to illustrate ease of use and run it continuously at the point of sale in shops.
5.  Sales Presentations. A video profile of a company to use as an introduction to new clients sells a company rather than products.
6.  Local News. There is potential in many areas for a local news magazine service on video, perhaps monthly. Make your tape, have copies made and rent it out through existing video shops.
7.  Amateur Theatrical Productions. You could record these and sell them as an entertainment.
8.  Your Own Video Programmes. There is no reason why a small video company cannot produce programmes and then sell or hire out the tapes through shops. Programmes such as 'How to Build a Home Extension' or 'Play Better Golf' could be very successful.

There is possibly even scope to produce subcontract programmes for television companies, though this would need specialist equipment and an experienced producer, so it is very much an idea for the future.

**Summary**
1. This is a venture for which you need some skill.
2. You need to sell the idea of your service heavily, as it will be new to most people.
3. Hire your equipment at first, and buy when you are more established.
4. There are many different fields in which a video film production business can operate.

---

## PROJECT 76: SCHOOL PHOTOGRAPHY

| | |
|---|---|
| *Status* | Mainly part-time, possibly full-time |
| *Capital required* | Low |
| *Return* | High, fast |
| *Can be combined with* | Projects 75 and 77 |

---

**Project facts**
One long-established business has gone through something of a decline in the past, but is now enjoying a revival with a new modern look. It is school photography. The concept of taking photographs of pupils and then selling them on approval to parents is not new, but imaginative forms of selling can make it more successful than previously. You can more than compete with existing school photographers — in the limited way that they still exist.

**What do I need?**
- Transport.
- Assistants (one or two).
- Equipment, including camera, lenses, lighting system and a back-drop curtain. Seek advice from a camera shop if you have no knowledge.
- Some photographic skill. Attend a course in portrait photography if necessary.
- Processing facilities. Agree with a local laboratory (look under **Photographic Processors** in the Yellow Pages) to process your work.
- The professional association is the British Institute of Professional Photography, 2 Amwell End, Ware, Herts.
- Background information on photography can be obtained from *Camera Choice* and *Camera and Creative Photography* (available at newsagents), and the *British Journal of Photog-*

*raphy* (a trade journal available at main libraries).

- Information on possible school customers can be gained from *Education Directory and Annual* or *The Parents' Guide to Independent Schools* (published by SFIA Educational Trust, 10 Queen Street, Maidenhead, Berkshire). Both these are available at main libraries.

## Pros and cons

| Pros | Cons |
|------|------|
| An established service which you can break into by being competitive | The 'on approval' service means a risk of not breaking even if photos do not sell |
| You can obtain valuable repeat orders year after year | |

## How do I operate?

In the past this service was sold mostly to the school in general, with revenue going to school funds. Now, however, the tendency is to sell to a group within the school, perhaps providing cash for a special purpose. Approach suitable groups at schools, eg the school camera club, sports club, parent-teacher association or fete committee. In some cases a pupil council or perhaps the school sixth form would be interested.

The concept behind approaching groups is that they will be more interested than the school as a whole. The project will perhaps earn them money for a particular need. They can also clear the idea with the school head and provide all the in-school organisation and administration.

To start, call schools at random from the telephone directory, whether state or private. A school secretary can usually point you in the direction of a society or group. Explain your idea, offer them a commission, negotiating as necessary to get the deal.

Go to the school as arranged and set up your equipment in a convenient place. It is then the responsibility of your contact to get every pupil before the camera over a fairly short period. It can be a good idea to get permission for pupils to be photographed wearing 'ordinary' clothes, not the usual uniform. Such photographs are far more popular with pupils and, evidence suggests, with parents too.

When you have taken the photographs, all negative stock needs to be forwarded to your processors. It's usual to produce about four different colour prints (in two different sizes). Place these in a clear bag accompanied by card mounts (obtainable from a wholesaler) and an explanatory sales letter. Photographs are then distributed to pupils via your school contacts. It's usual to offer the photographs on approval, that is, on a sale-or-return basis. This involves an element of risk, but units bought will invariably both pay for and outweigh units returned.

Individually, profits are not enormous. But you can repeat the procedure over and over again from school to school and year to year. It would even be possible to operate at a loss in the first year in order to profit from repeat orders in future years.

## Summary

1. If you do not already have some photographic knowledge, it is advisable to attend a course.
2. Sell your service to a group within each school, rather than to the school as a whole. It is the responsibility of your contact to ensure that all pupils are there. The group then gets a commission on your sales.
3. When you have taken the photographs, send them for processing, producing four different prints in two sizes.
4. Send these, with mounts, to your contact for distribution.
5. Some will be returned, but the ones that sell should more than pay for the ones that don't.

## PROJECT 77: STREET PHOTOGRAPHY

| | |
|---|---|
| *Status* | Part-time mostly, full-time in peak season |
| *Capital required* | Very low |
| *Return* | Very high, short-term |
| *Can be combined with* | Projects 75 and 76 |

## Project facts

Street photography has been 'rescued' from the past with good effect. It simply involves visiting areas popular with tourists (such as seaside resorts) with a cut-out photographic model board, then taking photographs and collecting the money. It is ideal for a part-time, sideline money spinner.

## What do I need?

- A good quality camera and tripod.
- Basic photographic skills.
- Advertising posters.
- A cut-out model board.

- Possibly assistants.
- Possibly a street trading licence.

## Pros and cons

| Pros | Cons |
|---|---|
| Very low investment | Irregular, occasional income |
| Easy to set up | |

## How do I operate?

Check with the local authority, whether you need a licence. To start, you need a cut-out model board. You may have seen the sort of thing before — a 'fat lady' in a bathing costume with hole cut for the head, or a policeman, a clown or an astronaut. This can be constructed from plywood supported by a timber frame so that it stands upright.

You could employ part-timers to operate this system, perhaps students in summer, so that a number of boards can be operated in a given area, each a different model.

The operators travel the area with the boards soliciting custom by calling to the crowd, or by advertisement boards. Sales are very much made on an impulse basis. The idea is a novelty from the past that large numbers of people would find fun. Each customer simply slips their head through the board and a photograph is taken. The assistants fill out a simple order form noting the photograph number and address of the customer, and take the payment, in the region of £5.

At the end of the day the photographs are developed (use a local chemist) mounted on a smart card and posted to the customer. It all adds up to a high-earning novelty of the sort that is especially popular in holiday and tourist areas.

## Summary

1. Check whether you need a licence.
2. Make a cut-out model board, or more than one if you intend operating on more than one pitch.
3. Travel the area soliciting custom either by simply calling to the crowd, or by means of an advertising board.
4. When you have taken a photograph, write out an order, making a note of the customer's name and address, and taking payment.
5. When the film is processed, post the photographs to the customer.

# PROJECT 78: A POSTCARD PHOTO LIBRARY

| | |
|---|---|
| *Status* | Part-time, full-time later |
| *Capital required* | Low |
| *Return* | Good, but long-term |
| *Can be combined with* | Projects 77 and 79 |

## Project facts
A camera can act as the basis for many businesses. One is
in supplying photographs for postcards, calendars and the like.
Thousands of photographs are bought annually for such products,
many from amateurs. Your advantage is that you can produce the
product cheaply and easily. If you fail to sell your work, very little
is lost, yet a couple of photographs sold and published can result
in an excellent return for the work.

## What do I need?
* A good camera and a selection of lenses and film. One can be
  bought second-hand for less than £100. Tell a camera shop that
  you wish mainly to photograph views (which most postcards
  are) and they will advise you accordingly.
* Some photographic skill.
* Trade associations are the British Institute of Professional
  Photography, 2 Amwell End, Ware, Hertfordshire SG12
  9HN, and the British Association of Picture Libraries, PO Box
  284, London W11 4RP.
* The *Directory of British Photographic Collections*, published
  by Heinemann, is a good reference.
* The *Writers' and Artists' Yearbook* is an essential first contact.

## Pros and cons
| Pros | Cons |
|---|---|
| Income can be considerable for successful photographs | May take time to establish |
| | Your products must suit buyers' requirements exactly |

## How do I operate?
The aim should be to build up your own photo library. Take
a shot of any and every subject you can. In this way, you are
sure to take a number of photographs that will appeal to buyers.
If you are not an experienced photographer, it is advisable to take
an evening class.

Remember that most postcards and calendars are views of some kind, whether coast or country, a castle or a monument. So concentrate on this type of photograph. There will be ample opportunities in your own area, but you can make research trips to other areas — holidays are the ideal opportunity.

It is better to take a photo, then reject it, than to skimp on your library. So keep all the shots you take. A library of about 200 is a minimum to start.

Next research the market. There are many publishers of postcards, calendars and greetings cards who use photographs. Some products are illustrated with photographs (like chocolate boxes), and many magazines need postcard-type photographs. Details of potential users and agencies can be found in press directories or the *Writers'& Artists' Yearbook*.

The best way to sell your service is by writing to potential buyers. Explain your service, offer samples and list your library stock. Treat positive replies carefully. Send copies of three or four of your best photographs, plus a complete list (a short description only) of all the rest. Whether sending clients samples or orders, it is customary to send transparencies of either 5in x 4in or 3¼in x 2¼in for consideration. 35mm slides are rarely welcome. Always send return postage for work sent on approval.

When photographs are accepted, negotiate the fee and terms. Some buyers have a flat fee, but this can sometimes be negotiated. Consider the type, quality and volume of the product in question. In all cases, buyers may only use your work once for a specific agreed purpose. If they want to use it again a further fee is payable, but you would probably have to agree not to resell the photograph to anyone else in the near future. Fee negotiation is an important part of this activity. Some small users may pay only a few pounds. Others may offer hundreds for what is quite a simple shot.

## Summary
1. A good camera is essential, and so is some skill at using it.
2. Approach only established buyers and submit samples in accepted formats.
3. Negotiate a suitable fee, taking into account the quality.
4. Be prepared for failures and balance them with successes.

## PROJECT 79: A COMPLETE PHOTO LIBRARY

| | |
|---|---|
| *Status* | Part-time/full-time |
| *Capital required* | Low |
| *Return* | Potentially very high |

### In brief

**Project 78** is an excellent way of cashing in with a camera. The business generated will be small, but good rewards are possible for a few photographs. For the advanced photographer, however, there is potential to operate a full-scale library which could develop into a major business.

This sort of business would operate in exactly the same way as a postcard library, but many more photographs would be required, perhaps around 1,000 to start (ideally 2,500). These can all be taken by you, but a simpler method is to buy some in from good amateur photographers for a couple of pounds each. Try to concentrate on half a dozen subjects, for example, animals, vehicles or architecture.

The main advantage of a larger library is the much larger range of customers. Promote your service to newspapers, magazines, book publishers, advertising agencies, product manufacturers and television stations. When they need a certain photograph for a certain purpose within your specialities, you can negotiate a high fee for quick supply.

This business may take time to grow. You need to establish a respected name in the trade, but it is one way by which a simple photo can make a very desirable product indeed.

Researching possible buyers is a must before expending time and money taking and purchasing library projects. Consult the variety of press and media publications you will find at main libraries.

Further details on how to proceed are given in **Project 78.**

# PROJECT 80: PLANT RENTAL

| | |
|---|---|
| *Status* | Full-time/part-time |
| *Capital required* | Low to Moderate |
| *Return* | Good, long-term |
| *Can be combined with* | Projects 81 and 90 |

## Project facts

In business, the promotion of a professional appearance is increasingly important, yet many firms do not have the time to attend to this aspect. So considerable demand has developed for services that help keep business appearances up.

One of the foremost public relations demands is for attractive-looking premises. This can be achieved with well-planned plant displays, all supplied and maintained on a rental basis! This idea is already established, but offers more scope for exploitation. It is a good business for enthusiasts, requiring little capital but offering good and regular rewards.

## What do I need?

- A knowledge of houseplants and their cultivation.
- A stock of plants.
- Transport.
- The ability to sell your service.
- *Nurseryman & Garden Centre* is a useful trade journal, and *Garden News* and *Practical Gardening* may give background information.
- A magazine like *House and Garden* will give ideas for plants in interior design.

## Pros and cons

| Pros | Cons |
|---|---|
| Once established, income is regular for very little work | Needs time to build up plant stock |
| Style and design is becoming more important in business | Sales effort must be continuous and quite high-pressured |

## How do I operate?

Get to know about house plants if you are not already knowledgeable. Alternatively make contact with an enthusiastic amateur who can advise you. Build up a stock of plants. Seeds and plants for growing on can be bought from a nursery and propagated in a heated greenhouse or warm, light room. There are no restrictions on the plants you can use, and any book on indoor plants will advise on their cultivation.

Next, sell your service. There is quite a demand from businesses who take appearances seriously. Professional offices (accountants, solicitors etc) are a good source of customers but there are many more. Write sales letters or (better still) sell in person. Enter into an agreement with customers to provide well-maintained, ever-changing plant displays in the office. Arrange a regular payment (say £5 – £10 per week per display). Many offices have room for several.

Create an attractive display. Use tubs or troughs filled with potting compost and a good display of plants. Be creative in arranging them, but ensure that they are placed according to their needs. Arrange for someone to water them as necessary — a secretary can usually be asked to do this. Once a month (or every two months) return to change the display. This can be done by exchanging plants with other offices. Discard dying plants and introduce new ones as necessary.

It is important to keep a high standard of display as this is a business where customers will recommend you to colleagues. You can also expand indefinitely, maybe employing people with 'green fingers' (and a van) to run rounds for you, while you concentrate on selling to new customers.

**Summary**
1. If you don't already have a basic knowledge of houseplant cultivation, you will need to read up on the subject.
2. Build up a good stock of plants.
3. Sell your service by letter or by personal visit.
4. Create an attractive display and change it every month or two.
5. Customer satisfaction is important, as business can be gained by personal recommendation.

---

## PROJECT 81: INTERIOR DESIGN

| | |
|---|---|
| *Status* | Part-time, could be full-time |
| *Capital required* | Low |
| *Return* | Very high, long-term |
| *Can be combined with* | Projects 49, 80 and 90 |

---

**Project facts**
In some businesses the product you sell is not anything tangible,

but an idea. That's just the case with interior design. Some customers pay thousands of pounds for the advice of a professional designer when that advice is just based upon imaginative ideas and product knowledge — knowledge you can pick up reasonably easily.

An interest in home decoration and furnishing is a help, but you need not be an expert to start. Promotional cash, transport and the ability to present your ideas are the main requirements.

## What do I need?
- Imaginative design ideas and the ability to visualise them in a particular setting.
- The ability to present and 'sell' your ideas.
- Cash to promote your service.
- Transport.
- The professional association is the British Institute of Interior Design, 1c Devonshire Avenue, Beeston, Nottingham NG9 1BS.
- The Design Council, 28 Haymarket, London SW1Y 4SU (Tel.01-839 8000), produces useful information on well-designed products.
- A useful annual reference guide is *Decorative Art and Modern Interiors,* available from main libraries.
- Magazines to consult include *Homes and Gardens, House and Garden* and *Ideal Home.*

## Pros and cons

| Pros | Cons |
|---|---|
| You can charge very high fees for this service | To do really well, you need a 'flair' |
| Very little initial outlay is necessary | Takes some time to become known |

## How do I operate?
Subscribe to all the magazines you can find on home care, decorating and design. A number of magazines for women cover these subjects in detail. Also obtain back copies where possible and get to know about all the latest fashions and products in interior design. A number of colleges offer design courses.

Next, contact manufacturers and suppliers who advertise in these magazines. Ask for current brochures on their products and services, and ask to be kept informed on new ideas and ranges. In a matter of weeks you can assemble a good research library of material to base your business on.

With basic skills you can set about getting commissions. The best customers to aim at are domestic, but you can also branch out into shop and office interiors. The most effective way to advertise is in the Yellow Pages. To start, you could get business through advertising in county magazines and other quality journals.

The accent in this service should be to undertake a small number of commissions for high fees — £30 or more per hour of your time. This is therefore not a service that you can successfully promote in the mass market. Repeat and recommendation trade from satisfied clients is important, and commissions worth several thousand pounds at a time are possible.

When you receive a commission arrange an 'input session' with the client. The idea of this is to weigh up the room to be designed and also the tastes of the client in furnishings, colours etc. In most cases the client will tell you what sort of atmosphere they wish to create. It is up to you to create a design to suit their personal tastes. This is very much up to your imagination — there is no right or wrong!

Start with a rough outline of your ideas. Then consult your resource material to give them some substance. The best way is to start with basics — ceilings, walls etc — before moving on to lighting, floor covering, curtains or furniture. Main libraries will have books on home design which can help with both theory and practice, but your own library of books would be better in the longer term.

When you have decided on a design draw it up as professionally as you can. Your drawings needn't be exact, nor to scale, but they should communicate your ideas. Make your proposals look professional with colour and fabric samples, magazine and brochure cuttings and photographs wherever necessary.

Finally, present this report to the customer for final clearance — 'fine tuning' to their tastes if necessary. Occasionally you might have completely misinterpreted their needs and have to start again from scratch. Generally though, clients are interested in your ideas and impressions and will find them acceptable.

For a starter business you can end your service here, and leave it to the client to arrange for the work to be done. For useful extra income though, arrange with suitable specialists to decorate and furnish the room and claim a fee of about 10% of the cost of their work on top of your design charges.

What you do will depend on the nature of the design. But you might for example have an electrician instal new 'mood effect' lighting, then retain a decorator to paint and wallpaper the room, then choose and have carpets laid and curtains hung by a specialist shop. Finally, you might personally supervise the purchase and arrangement of all the trimmings — the ornaments, paintings, sculpture that make the room special. This is where you can cash in on your own imagination!

## How much can I earn?

**Example:** An actual small interior design service reports limited but healthy demand in the rural area they service. Their commissions include the redesign of a small coffee shop interior for £400, up to the complete design and refurbishment of a weekend country cottage. Fees for this were £1,800 plus a 5% commission on the cost of the work (payment for organising it) at £5,300.

## Summary

1. Build up a research library from magazines, books and manufacturers' brochures.
2. Advertise in county magazines and other quality journals.
3. This is an 'up-market' service, so a professional approach is essential.
4. When you receive a commission, discuss the client's ideas and preferences with them.
5. Get ideas from your research library and put together a plan, with samples of materials and colours to be used, for the client's approval.
6. Your role can stop there, but you can also undertake to oversee the actual work, making arrangements with suitable specialists.

---

# PROJECT 82: JEWELLERY MAKING

| | |
|---|---|
| *Status* | Part-time/full-time |
| *Capital required* | Low |
| *Return* | High |
| *Can be combined with* | Projects 10 and 83 |

---

## Project facts

Jewellery is one of the oldest hand crafts and ideal as a new business activity. Beautiful pieces can be created from inexpensive parts in a home workshop then sold on at the high margins invariably attached to this sort of product.

There are no special requirements for this activity, save an interest in the subject, an eye for detail and a careful, steady hand. Capital requirement can start at £25 and no technical knowledge is necessary.

## What do I need?
- A supply of materials.
- A careful, steady hand.
- A few basic skills.
- A useful journal is *Gems and Mineral Realm*.
- The 'trade association' is the British Crafts Centre, 43 Earlham Street, London WC2H 9LD.

## Pros and cons
| Pros | Cons |
|---|---|
| Needs no technical knowledge | Could take time to build up |
| Very little capital required | |

## How do I operate?
Before starting you will need a supply of components, such as semi-precious gems. They are much easier to get hold of than you might expect. There are a number of specialist suppliers of inexpensive jewellery-making materials. Locate them through small ads in craft magazines at your newsagents or library.

Most suppliers have a catalogue they will supply on request. Obtain a selection of these brochures to see the range of semi-precious stones and accessories available. This includes everything from gold and silver (often plated) ring mounts, earrings, chains and pendants to diamonds, sapphires and emeralds. Many suppliers have a sample package of parts you can buy inexpensively to experiment with the skills.

The first step is to decide on designs. Many suppliers have patterns for particular pieces with instructions you can follow. It is probably best to devise a range of about fifteen different pieces including rings, earrings and necklaces at least, and any other items you want to make.

Secondly, buy in parts for the jewellery lines. You can match the quality of stones and accessories to the amount of capital available for investment, but obviously the cost of the parts will relate to the finished price.

Next, assemble the jewellery. Only basic skills like soldering, threading and fine tying are needed. Suppliers will provide all materials, instructions and craft manuals. For efficiency, work on a production line basis, or employ homeworkers working in their own homes and paid by the item.

Finally, pack them attractively. Boxes should be available from the material suppliers. You now have an attractive, desirable product. Although it tends to be of a lower quality and price compared with 'shop' jewellery there are many outlets, such as:

- jewellers' shops selling budget lines
- market traders
- a market stall
- wholesalers (supplying market traders and small shops)
- arts and craft fairs
- mail order in newspapers and magazines
- party plan, or to party plan traders
- your own discount jewellery shop

A wide variety of sales outlets can be used. Whichever you use remember that self-assembly jewellery tends to sell in the lower price bracket, frequently as fun or fashion jewellery. It is here that you should direct your sales effort.

## How much can I earn?
**Example:** One amateur home jeweller specialises in making inexpensive fashion earrings. Two imitation gemstones cost about 25p. Two mounts (either clips or studs) cost about 20p. A mounting card costs about 10p to have attractively gold-blocked. The total product cost is around 55p. There are many ways of selling, but this 'jeweller' principally sells to market traders and small fashion shops. She sells boxes of ten assorted pairs of earrings for £15. The retailer therefore makes a fair profit and the jeweller makes about £10 on a box of ten. Most weeks she makes and sells seven or eight boxes, but it has been as much as fifteen in an especially good week, still part-time.

## Summary
1. Find sources of supply for materials.
2. Decide on the designs you are going to use — many suppliers provide patterns.
3. Make the jewellery up according to the supplier's instructions.
4. Sell to outlets other than jewellery shops, such as market traders or through mail order.

## PROJECT 83: JUNK JEWELLERY

| | |
|---|---|
| *Status* | Mostly part-time |
| *Capital required* | Very low |
| *Return* | Moderate |

### In brief

There is an opportunity to start in jewellery at an even lower level than self-assembly. This is to design and make junk jewellery — as the name implies made from 'junk', and all the more fashionable for this reason!

It can be made from virtually anything. Metal nuts, washers, coins, chain and brass or copper wire can be used. Pieces of wood, wooden rings, beads and pieces of string are also possibilities. Design your products, whether they be necklaces, bracelets, rings or earrings, on paper first then make them up. Wholesale ironmongers can be a good source of parts. For better-quality pieces incorporate stones and other items.

The market is more restricted than for 'ordinary' jewellery, but still quite wide and profitable. Try fashion shops, boutiques, kiosks and market traders. Some of the lower-priced regular jewellers might be interested in some of your better pieces.

This opportunity is very much a small-scale, owner-operated activity, though there is potential to expand to a full-time business of not inconsiderable size. Design and research is important. Experiment with designing and making your own pieces. For a larger business finance talented art, design or craft students from a local school or college to do this for you. Contact such people through newspaper advertisements.

## PROJECT 84: IDEAS FOR GAMES

| | |
|---|---|
| *Status* | Part-time, occasional only |
| *Capital required* | Very low |
| *Return* | High, but uncertain |
| *Can be combined with* | Project 73 |

### Project facts

There are often considerable sums to be made just from, ideas. A unique opening is the inventing of games and puzzles.

*Creative & Artistic Businesses*

Interesting opportunities exist here for anyone with imagination. Such a venture does not offer a predictable income. It is more a 'nothing or everything' business. It is therefore ideal as a sideline activity.

## What do I need?
- Ideas for games or puzzles.
- The ability to sell them.
- *Manufacturers and Merchants Directory* (available at main libraries) is a good source of games manufacturers.
- The trade journal is *Toy Trader*.

## Pros and cons

| Pros | Cons |
| --- | --- |
| Very simple ideas can be very profitable | Very much a speculative project |
| Royalties worth millions of pounds are possible if your idea succeeds | No guaranteed income possible |

## How do I operate?
Prepare a personal file of game and puzzle manufacturers. Some are major national names. Others are smaller makers or agents. Apart from the UK, consider European and Far East manufacturers too. The American market is enormous and this is where your best chances may be. The appeal of such products today is truly international and offering your ideas overseas is quite practical. Find contact names on existing products. Most boxes carry the manufacturers' addresses.

Devise your games proposals. This is very much a matter of personal taste. You might go for a card game, some sort of three-dimensional puzzle, or a board game in the style of something like Monopoly. Write your proposals down and include sketches.

Write an introductory letter to the manufacturers. Have letters professionally typed and presented. Ask if they are interested in new ideas. Most will at least consider them, as long as they are not obviously based on an existing game. Send a list of your best ideas explaining each in no more than about 500 words.

If a manufacturer is interested prepare a mock-up of the game with instructions etc, and take it personally to the manufacturer if it is a UK company, for a demonstration. Be prepared for failures and persist, offering new games to the same manufacturer and rejected games to other manufacturers. If you are successful, a manufacturer will produce the game and pay you a royalty. Take legal advice to ensure that any agreement made is fair.

Your efforts may well not pay off, but you could be very well rewarded in royalties if a game is accepted, even more so if it becomes a best seller!

## Summary

1. Make up a file of game and puzzle manufacturers, and the sort of products they specialise in.
2. When you have thought of an idea for a game, write to manufacturers, asking if they are interested in new ideas. Send a description in about 500 words.
3. If a manufacturer expresses interest, prepare a mock-up and take it to the manufacturer for a demonstration.
4. If you are successful, you will be paid a royalty on sales. Get legal advice on any contract before signing.

# PROJECT FILE 5
## Self-Managing Businesses

These are businesses which require a minimum of supervision on your part. They will more or less run themselves. You simply act as manager — and collect the money! They will therefore appeal to people who have a job or business already, but want an attractive sideline for a bit of extra money.

## PROJECT 85: DOOR-TO-DOOR CATALOGUE SALES

| | |
|---|---|
| *Status* | Part-time |
| *Capital required* | Moderate |
| *Return* | Quick, short-term. |
| *Can be combined with* | Projects 51, 52 and 70 |

### Project facts

Methods of retailing change little over the years, but every so often, a new one comes along. One of the latest developments is in door-to-door catalogue selling. This has been tried on a limited basis in some areas and shows excellent potential for expansion in the coming years. Door-to-door catalogue sales mix the advantages of mail order with a degree of personal service.

### What do I need?

- Some capital for advertising literature.
- A telephone.
- Good persuasive and negotiating skills.

### Pros and cons

| Pros | Cons |
|---|---|
| Catalogue buying has proved popular | Needs considerable negotiating skills |
| There are no stock overheads | |

### How do I operate?

This kind of business was started by a furniture retailer in a small town. He had a loyal clientele but had great difficulty in attracting new customers to his showrooms. To solve the problem he decided to create a colour catalogue of his best items of occasional furniture and distribute it door-to-door.

To make the catalogue of more interest he approached other shops selling household goods, gifts and the like and arranged to include their products in the catalogue. In return, each shop owner would pay him a 10% commission on any item sold and undertake to deliver the item to the door of the buyer.

The initial printing and distribution of 10,000 catalogues was an enormous success, selling healthy quantities of both his own furniture and other home and gift lines. It seemed customers enjoyed shopping from a catalogue, but were more ready to buy because they could telephone and have the item delivered. The extra convenience meant customers would pay extra, even if they could buy the same item from other shops.

A similar project could be copied in most areas or regions small or large. There is no need to concentrate on any specific trade if you can find suitable sources of supply. Just decide on a range of products — anything for the home is suitable. Contact local shops, explain your idea, and offer to include their goods in your brochure for a commission.

Make up a professional catalogue of at least twenty items. Have full descriptions and photographs if possible. Contact a firm of designers and a colour printer to do this. Look under **Designers, Advertising & Graphic** and **Printers** in the Yellow Pages. Distribute it to local houses, using a distribution firm, or drop in with local free newspapers.

Set up a 'telephone hotline' to take orders. Your home telephone will do to start on a small scale. Relay orders to suppliers daily. They deliver (for which they can charge), collect payment, and forward commission to you.

You can expand by covering other local areas, changing the product range frequently, and repeating offers regularly to areas which show average or above average response.

This is a particularly interesting retail project set to create a great deal of interest in the next few years. One of the great advantages is that it can be tested at very low cost with minimal resources. Should it fail little is lost. Where it works it can be expanded readily as resources permit. Once order levels become established supplies of goods can be bought straight from manufacturers for extremely large profit margins.

## Summary

1. Decide on a range of products — preferably household ones.
2. Approach local shops offering to include their goods in your catalogue for a commission.
3. Make up a colourful catalogue, and have it distributed throughout the area.
4. Set up a system for receiving telephone orders, and relay them to your suppliers.
5. Once the business becomes established, you can buy goods direct from manufacturers.

# PROJECT 86: MAIL ORDER

| | |
|---|---|
| *Status* | Part-time/full-time |
| *Capital required* | Moderate |
| *Return* | Potentially high, fast |

## In brief

The catalogue sales opportunity is a good way of testing products locally, but you can then expand into a national network. The way to do this is through mail order. Mail order is a unique sales technique, and there are very few goods that can't be sold by this method. Start in mail order in exactly the same way as door-to-door catalogue sales — with suitable products. Furniture and furnishing products are ideal, but you will need a much greater profit margin for mail order selling, at least 100% if possible. Approach wholesalers or importers.

Prepare your catalogue using the very highest standard of print and presentation you can afford. Advertise in suitable publications. For example, home furnishings or clothes could sell well in magazines for women. Catalogues are then despatched to enquirers and subsequent orders collated by you and forwarded to the suppliers. Unlike local sales the delivery cost will be greater and should be allowed for in the overall price.

Mail order is a rather more technical business than local sales. You must test the potential for products in small advertisements before spending a great deal. Cut your losses on unsuccessful products, capitalise on successful ones. One way of doing this is to advertise proven successful products in Sunday colour supplement magazines. A quarter of a page can cost several thousand pounds, but can be repaid many times over.

Mail order is also highly dependent on repeat sales. Existing customers must be continually mailed with new offers in order to make advertising pay satisfactorily.

The business does require further study, but in many ways it follows the concept of catalogue sales and in company with that can be tried at modest cost. Mail order has long been offered as a traditional business opportunity but when considered as a method of selling and not a business in its own right it stands a much greater chance of success.

The Mail Order Traders Association is at 507 Corn Exchange Building, Fenwick Street, Liverpool L2 7RA (Tel.051-236 7581).

The British Direct Marketing Association is at 1 New Burlington Street, London W1X 1FD (Tel. 01-437 4485).

A valuable, though rather technical, book for anyone trading by mail order is the *Direct Mail and Mail Order Handbook* by Richard S. Hodgson, published by the Dartnell Corporation and widely available in public libraries.

Details of catalogue production etc are given in **Project 85**.

## PROJECT 87: A BUSINESS SERVICES BUREAU

| | |
|---|---|
| *Status* | Part-time to start |
| *Capital required* | Low |
| *Return* | Moderate |
| *Can be combined with* | Projects 30, 31, 34 and 88 |

### Project facts
This is a project which helps other businesses. Almost every small and medium-sized business would welcome a competent bureau they could use full or part time, whether for a relief typing service, or for regular book-keeping. Such agencies do exist, but those using truly professional staff are few and far between. A business services bureau offers a professional service but at reasonable rates.

### What do I need?
- Good-quality staff.
- A professional approach.
- The journals *British Business* and *In Business Now* will provide information on the world of small business.

### Pros and cons
**Pros**

Can provide a good income for just some organisational input

**Cons**

There is competition

### How do I operate?
Good staff are the key to this business. You must only recruit professionally trained and experienced secretarial staff, not self-taught people like some bureaux. However, part-timers are ideally suited. Advertise for staff in local newspapers or through Job Centres. Interview applicants to determine their competence, then establish

your 'register of skills'. You should be able to offer services like typing, word processing, book-keeping, telephone answering, telephone sales and computer operation.

Advertise the service locally. Use the local press, letters and personal or telephone calls to possible customers. Most businesses locally could have some need for help with office work. Emphasise the professionalism of your staff over other agencies. Offer to provide services on either a full- or part-time basis. Agree fees — the standard rate for the job (consult Job Centres) plus a 30% commission for you.

Once set up, much of the work is organisational. You accept work from the customer, transmit it to your employee, and return it when the job is completed. Invoice the customer weekly, but pay the employee only monthly for a smooth cash flow. Much of the work can be carried out by the employees in their own homes with their equipment. Alternatively they can work at the customer's premises. The first alternative is ideal for helping businesses out at busy periods. The second provides a useful relief staff service.

Such a service is nothing new, but quality and standard of work and organisation are the important factors that will lessen competition for your service.

## Summary

1. Run only a quality service using competent, trained staff.
2. Transmit all work through your business, not direct between the customer and the employee. The latter may be considered an employment agency which requires a licence.
3. Offer modern techniques. Many bureaux cannot compete on this point.

## PROJECT 88: A COMPUTER BUREAU

| | |
|---|---|
| *Status* | Part-time/full-time |
| *Capital required* | Medium to high |
| *Return* | Moderate but steady |

### In brief

Many business functions nowadays are based on computers, so offering some computerised services — either in addition to other business services, or on their own — can be lucrative.

The main requirement is a computer, but a personal computer is adequate to start. Consult a specialist computer centre. There are several powerful machines available with monitors, keyboards, printers and disc drives. Software programmes are available too. Budget for about £1,000, half for the machine, half for the software.

Alternatively, one way to start this business with far less investment is to employ outside computer owners as and when you have work available. Many people have quite sophisticated home computers for hobby purposes and would welcome occasional work to help finance their computer hobby. Place advertisements in local newspapers in order to contact them. By operating in this way you build a business which you can run with the minimum of work. Your main task is to obtain the work and pass it on to the most suitable computer operator.

Most computers can be operated by beginners, but courses are available and frequently advertised in newspapers. In spite of this many small and medium-sized businesses do not have computers and would be interested in the service. Start part-time and build to full time as customers increase. Services to offer include:

- daily correspondence, letters, enquiries, invoices
- word processing, quick production of error-free documents
- compilation and preparation of mailing lists
- purchase and sales ledger accounting
- wages and salaries
- management accounts
- Value Added Tax

If necessary, consult an accountant to advise on accounting techniques.

This is one activity where you can start in a very basic way, and develop the service as you gain more experience. For example, one computer service started with a simple home word-processing service for business letters. It eventually expanded to offering a personalised mailshot facility for mail order companies with an annual turnover of £550,000!

Find out demand for such a service locally. The *What Micro?* series of publications (available at main libraries) will help in your choice of a computer and computer system if required.

## PROJECT 89: A PRINTER'S JOBBER

| | |
|---|---|
| *Status* | Part-time, later full-time |
| *Capital required* | Very low |
| *Return* | Good, commission basis |
| *Can be combined with* | Projects 45, 46 and 87 |

### Project facts

Many businesses make their money by 'broking' something between buyer and seller. The term is more usually associated with insurance, but the concept exists in other areas where little or no product knowledge is required to make money.

An ideal example of this is print broking. The printer's jobber, as he is known, takes printing orders from a client, then finds the cheapest possible supplier to supply the order. He does no printing himself, but makes a generous commission for saving the customer money and getting the printer work.

### What do I need?

- A few pounds (£20 or so) for advertising.
- A telephone.
- For background information, consult the magazines *British Printer* and *Printing World*.
- The *Printing Trades Directory* and *Printing Annual* are directories of printers.
- The trade associations are the Institute of Printing, 8 Lonsdale Gardens, Tunbridge Wells, Kent and British Printing Industries Federation, 11 Bedford Row, London, WC1R 4DX.

### Pros and cons

| Pros | Cons |
|---|---|
| Profit margins can be very high in some cases | Printing is a competitive industry |
| There is a chance to take enormous commissions on large orders for very little work | |

### How do I operate?

First, sell your service. Advertise in the same way as a printer in local newspapers. More experienced jobbers often open a small office in a business or commercial area. Emphasise you offer the lowest prices on any type of work. Printer's jobbers compete on efficient service and a wider range of printing types than sole printers. They can invariably undertake both large and small jobs, and offer all the most modern printing services. A jobber gets work on giving the very best value for money.

When a jobber obtains a request for a quotation for printing he then sets out to get the lowest possible quote. This is done by approaching a number of suitable printers. Select printers to approach from the Yellow Pages, working on a nationwide basis if necessary. A phone call will determine whether the printer can help. If so, discuss the customer's requirements and ask the printer to submit a written quotation by return. Always obtain about four or five quotes for any job.

Next, select the cheapest quote and, after adding a commission (around 10%) send a written quotation to the customer. If they accept, simply supply the order through the printer who submitted that quote. They take over the job from there on.

Clearly this procedure will be more difficult when you are new to the business, but it becomes much easier as you gain contacts in the industry. When printers realise you are a jobber and will give them regular work in return for keen prices they may well offer additional discounts, making your prices to customers even more competitive.

When working as a jobber it is vital to do no printing yourself. To do so would destroy the 'no work' advantage. By offering a good wide-ranging service at low prices you can more than compete with local printers.

## How much can I earn?

**Example:** A customer requires 5,000 copies of a four-colour sales brochure. The best price he gets from the local printer is £845.00 + VAT. The jobber obtains quotes of £600, £673, £750, £820 and £865 + VAT. He quotes the customer £750 + VAT based on the lowest price, and the customer then orders.

The customer orders for £750, the jobber orders for £600 and negotiates a 5% jobber's discount (so the actual price is £570.) The jobber is paid £750 by the customer, and pays £570 to printer. His mark up is £180, yet the customer saves £95 (all excluding VAT).

## Summary
1.  Advertise your services in local newspapers as if you were a printer.

2. Emphasise that you can offer the lowest price for any job.
3. When you get a request for a quotation, telephone printers around the country, and get four or five quotes.
4. Choose the cheapest, add 10% commission, and send your own quote to the customer.
5. When printers know you are a jobber and could give them extra work, they will often offer you an additional discount.

---

## PROJECT 90: PICTURE RENTAL

| | |
|---|---|
| *Status* | Mostly part-time |
| *Capital required* | Moderate |
| *Return* | Good, regular |
| *Can be combined with* | Project 80 |

---

### Project facts

Impressions are important in business nowadays. Large numbers of business people realise that attractive-looking premises reap rewards in terms of professional image. This has produced a demand for a lucrative sideline business in 'decor rental'.

One of the proven branches of this trade is in oil painting rental. You rent out oil paintings to professional offices in return for a regular charge. The customer benefits from smart premises, yet never owns the item. You get to benefit from a regular income.

### What do I need?

- A little cash to stock up with paintings.
- Transport.
- The ability to explain and persuade people to accept a new idea.
- The journal *The Artist* will provide some background on art appreciation, and the journal *Design* will give useful interior design tips.

### Pros and cons

| Pros | Cons |
|---|---|
| A growth area | Becoming quite competitive |
| Provides a regular income for little work | The supply of customers is limited |

## How do I operate?

Obtain a supply of framed original oil paintings, of all sizes and subjects. The cheapest way to do this is to buy from importers, where pictures are available from just £5 or so each. They advertise in import-export directories (available at libraries) or *Exchange & Mart*.

Write a sales letter explaining the service. Send a trial mailing of 500 or so to businesses with offices in your region (solicitors, accountants and similar professionals are ideal, but any business can be a customer). Visit any enquirers to explain your service.

Rent out a number of paintings to decorate the office. Charge a weekly rental (£2 – £5 or so) per painting. Visit the customer occasionally to swap paintings and create an ever-changing effect.

You can expand by signing up more and more customers for the service. £8 – £10 a week over 30 customers is excellent for the small amount of work involved. You can also offer sculptures or other items of decor.

## Summary

1. Obtain a supply of oil paintings from an importer.
2. Promote your service by means of a sales letter.
3. Any small business can be a potential customer, but the professions are a good bet.
4. Visit any enquirers and explain your service.
5. Charge a weekly rental for each painting, and change them occasionally.

## PROJECT 91: SUBDIVIDING OFFICE SPACE

| | |
|---|---|
| *Status* | Mostly part-time |
| *Capital required* | High |
| *Return* | Long-term |
| *Can be combined with* | Projects 26 and 92 |

## Project facts

With the growth in small businesses there is constant demand for small business accommodation. Large factories may stand empty, but in most areas small businesses still find it difficult to find compact and economical space. The problem is probably worst for office accommodation.

There is a solution to these important business needs that

can also make a great deal of money for the organiser. You lease a large area of office space and subdivide it for the sort of accommodation which is most in demand. You are in fact taking a commodity that no one wants and making it desirable, the principle of many good businesses.

## What do I need?
- Good negotiating skills.
- Local knowledge.
- Some capital to buy an initial lease.
- Source of legal advice.
- The *Estates Gazette* contains useful but technical information on property trends.

## Pros and cons

| Pros | Cons |
|---|---|
| Income can be very high | Large investment required |
| Virtually no work involved once it is set up | Takes a long time before any income is received |

## How do I operate?
Finding suitable space will not be a problem in most areas. The ideal sort of property is one previously occupied by a large company which has now moved to more modern premises, or perhaps closed down. The property need not be modern, but should be easily accessible from transport routes.

Find property through commercial estate agents (usually only in cities), and appropriate sections in major newspapers. Your local council may also be able to advise you. You are interested in any office space (or possibly workshop or shop space too) of between about 5,000 and 10,000 square feet.

First view the property. Check that it is suitable to be divided by simple plasterboard walls. Check that services such as electricity, water, telephone and parking are available. On the legal side check that there is planning consent (or it would be granted) for offices. Also ensure that the owners will allow you to sublet.

When you find a property get your solicitor to approach the owner. Offer to lease it for a minimum of five years. Offer them about 60% of the rent they ask for. (If you are not sure what a fair rent is ask a surveyor or valuer to advise you.) The whole idea behind this is that you are turning unpopular space into wanted space. So bold as your offer may seem, it does stand a good chance of being accepted. Larger office spaces can be difficult to let. It is cheaper for the owners to rent at something of a loss, than support an empty building. If you are not successful pull out of deals and keep negotiating until you find a favourable arrangement. Then get your solicitor to monitor the drawing up of the lease so as not to restrict your subletting.

Now you can divide your accommodation into convenient sizes. A typical business starter unit might be 15ft x 20ft, and you can offer larger firms two or three units joined together. If capital permits, have simple framework walls built between the units. If not, it is quite feasible to use screens or just paint lines on the floor! Individual businesses use lockers for the storage of any valuables.

You provide basic facilities like lighting, heating and toilets. The individual clients provide their own furniture, telephones and so on. For additional income you can employ a secretary to act as a telephonist, receptionist and typist, and provide photocopying and word processing facilities etc. Clients would pay for these as they use them on top of the rent.

With a little work you will have attractive office units ideal for small, new and growing businesses. Don't go to a lot of trouble because customers are looking for something cheap even if it means sharing with others. Having said this, rental income from ten 600 square foot units could well be three or four times that of a defunct 10,000 square foot one!

Advertise in local newspapers offering small business starter units. The demand will be anything from brisk to overpowering, depending on the area! Alternatively, employ a commercial estate agent as property managers. They will charge a fee, but will take care of everything from finding clients to collecting rent to employing someone to change the light bulbs!

Consult your solicitor about subletting, but generally it is best to let on a licence arrangement which has minimum formalities. Clients pay a fixed weekly rent which covers all costs. An absolute minimum notice period is required, which makes for a very flexible arrangement.

Keep running costs and administration to a minimum. A part-time caretaker can be retained for routine maintenance. Put regular maintenance, like cleaning communal areas, out to contract. Collect rent and pay bills as necessary. The aim is to keep the service (and the costs) to a bare minimum. This is what makes your accommodation attractive and makes the business very easy to run.

This sort of activity holds excellent potential as self-managing business. Once you have set up the units there is little else to do but routine administration — and collecting your rent. The activity is open-ended, virtually unlimited, and can expand to whatever size you want.

## How much can I earn?
Because small businesses are involved, individual rents are not enormous, but these all build up and could cover the rent you pay many times over.

**Example:** A manager had eight units let, paying £28 a week (£896 a month in total). He paid £300 a month to rent the whole complex. Most of his other bills were covered by the £80 a week profit from the on-site secretarial and catering service – serving both tenants and outside businesses.

## Summary
1.  Always consult a solicitor and surveyor before leasing any property.
2.  Find suitable space for subdividing through commercial estate agents or via your local council. Ensure that it has the necessary planning consent.
3.  Once you have agreed a lease with the owner of a property, subdivide it into smaller units, using simple walls, or just a painted line on the floor.
4.  You will need to provide heating,lighting and toilet facilities, but tenants will provide everything else.
5.  For extra income, you can provide secretarial, reception and photocopying services at an extra charge.

# PROJECT 92: SUBDIVIDING SHOP SPACE

| | |
|---|---|
| *Status* | Full-time or sideline |
| *Capital required* | High |
| *Return* | Possibly very high |

## In brief
The concept in **Project 91** offers excellent potential for expansion into retailing. In a similar way you could take a large, vacant shop unit and subdivide it into small units for letting to small traders.

Most town centres have a number of large vacant units, perhaps where chain stores and the like have expanded into modern shopping centres. These units of 15,000 square feet or more could be leased inexpensively, divided into units of 800 or so square feet with attractive walkways between them and relet. Alternatively, devise 'out of town' shopping centres in industrial units (subject to planning constraints).

This sort of opportunity requires more capital than offices and workshops, since retail rents tend to be higher and there is the additional expense of shopfitting, but the rents charged should compensate for this. Consult a local commercial estate agency for details of what you might charge.

With this scheme there is the potential to create attractive, popular mini-shopping centres. One scheme, for example, sublets 20 units to small clothes boutiques alone. Another contains assorted fast food outlets. A mixed centre, however, makes it easier to let.

Local knowledge helps very much here. First look out for suitable property through estate agents. Then discuss finances and feasibility with a solicitor and accountant.

Further details on how to proceed are given in **Project 91.**

# PROJECT 93: A COURIER SERVICE

| | |
|---|---|
| *Status* | Part-time/full-time |
| *Capital required* | Moderate to high |
| *Return* | Long-term |
| *Can be combined with* | Projects 15 and 23 |

## Project facts

Courier services for important items have long been a feature of large city life, but in the past these services have rarely existed in provincial areas. Very probably there is not enough demand to support full-time businesses, but there is certainly enough business for a part-time operation and a number of such organisations are starting up.

A courier service could be a much-needed new facility in many smaller city and town areas and is an idea where the market can be tested for very little outlay.

## What do I need?
- Transport, either motor cycle or car.
- Operators to work part time, perhaps with own transport.
- A telephone.
- Space for a 'control centre' at home.

- Cash for advertising.
- Possibly a licence.

## Pros and cons

| Pros | Cons |
|---|---|
| A much-needed service | Needs quite a lot of investment |
| Involves no complicated organisation | Can take time to get established |

## How do I operate?

First check that you do not require a licence.

The key point of the business is successful promotion of the service. This needs to be done intensively. Use local press advertising, mailshots and personal calls. Most customers will be local businesses. Offer fast delivery of documents and parcels in the region (set a limit of about 30 miles' radius).

Set a suitable rate for your services, usually on a mileage basis. The cost per mile to run most types of vehicle can be found in the reference pages of a magazine such as *What Car?* To this add a labour and profit mark up of about 120%.

Ensure that vehicles are insured for courier work, and carry no passengers as this would constitute a taxi service.

This business can be owner-operated, but it is easy to employ despatch riders, with their own transport, paid per job. Equip them with mobile radios, or keep in touch by telephone 'bleepers'. You will require a controller. His or her job is to take phone orders from customers and pass them on to the riders.

Keep careful records of journeys undertaken. This allows you to control your costs. Give genuine business customers the service on credit, then invoice them weekly.

This business is particularly simple and involves no complicated administration. However it is a business where efficiency and attention to detail will reap rewards. This applies particularly in those areas where the service is relatively new and able to fill a much-needed demand.

## How much can I earn?

**Example:** One small part-time courier service reports average weekly takings of £300 or so. About 50% of this goes to cover driver expenses and remuneration.

**Example:** Another in a major city has regular contracts worth around £700 per month, plus whatever casual work they can pick up.

## Summary

1. Check whether you need a licence.
2. Ensure vehicles are properly insured for courier work.
3. Promote the business extensively through press ads, mailshots and personal calls.
4. Charge by the mile.

# PROJECT 94: SANDWICH BOARD ADVERTISING

| | |
|---|---|
| *Status* | Mostly part-time |
| *Capital required* | Low |
| *Return* | Good, short-term |
| *Can be combined with* | Projects 2, 32, 45 and 46 |

## Project facts

Many modern businesses are based on some of the oldest ideas around. One such opportunity now starting to make a recovery is sandwich board advertising. Far from being a small-time activity this operation offers great potential in most towns and cities, where the sight of a walking advertisement could sell a wide range of things. This is ideal for an owner-operator or larger concern working from home and with minimal capital requirement.

## What do I need?

- Cheap boards.
- Operators.

## Pros and cons

| Pros | Cons |
|---|---|
| Virtually no investment | Income can be intermittent |

## How do I operate?

Have sandwich boards made cheaply by a local joiner. A basic board comprises two 18in x 36in boards held over the shoulder with leather straps. Three sets are ideal to start with.

Recruit operators through the local press. They will usually work part time, in shifts of three hours or so.

Get customers to advertise on the boards. Local businesses are the best bet. You can sell both products and services. It is ideal for restaurants, pubs and theatres but holds unlimited scope. Charge about four times what you pay the operators. Have posters painted by a poster artist at the customer's expense and pin them to the boards. An option is to hand out leaflet copies of the poster too.

Plan a route with each operator. It will usually be in the vicinity of the business being advertised, but it could be in the local town centre. Fancy dress is an optional extra to get more attention.

All that remains is to supervise the operators and recruit new advertisers as each job expires. If the business is operated part time then it would be a useful 'pin money' operation. However, there is certainly potential to operate a fleet of sandwich boards for a considerable, even if intermittent, advertising service.

### How much can I earn?

**Example:** One sandwich board service operates in the summer only in a major tourist town. They operate about twelve sandwich boards eight hours each day, paying operators about £2 per hour. Customers are charged £80 for a week's display, and their advertising message is displayed for about forty hours. The weekly income is around £1,920, wages and other expenses are around £960. But income would only be about half of this or less in winter.

### Summary
1. Have sandwich boards made by a local joiner, and recruit part-time operators through the local press.
2. Approach local businesses, especially restaurants, pubs and theatres, to advertise.
3. Have posters painted at the customer's expense.
4. Charge the customer twice what you pay the operators.

---

## PROJECT 95: A LANGUAGE SCHOOL

| | |
|---|---|
| *Status* | Part-time, possibly full-time |
| *Capital required* | Moderate |
| *Return* | Moderate, rising to high |
| *Can be combined with* | Project 1 |

---

### Project facts
As business becomes increasingly international the learning of foreign languages is a growing necessity. The traditional ways of learning are either evening classes or tapes. Both have advantages, but the general opinion is that neither is personalised nor specialist enough for most businessmen's needs.

The demand for better tuition has led to the development of

language schools offering a high standard of tuition for business people and the more serious holidaymakers. This is a field where there is potential for additional outlets.

## What do I need?

- Competent tutors – they may be members of the Institute of Linguists, 24a Highbury Grove, London N5 2EA (Tel. 01-359 7445) or the Translators' Association, 84 Drayton Gardens, London SW10 9SB (Tel. 01-373 6642).
- A venue.
- Organisational ability.

## Pros and cons

| Pros | Cons |
|---|---|
| Booming 'growth' market | You will almost certainly |
| Fees tend to be very high for business/executive customers | need to use staff |
| | You are reliant on the competence of others for the success of your business |

## How do I operate?

The basic need is for tutors for your course. The ease with which you can find them depends very much on the course you propose. An academic course would probably need a suitably qualified lecturer. However, modern language courses are very practical and don't require literary excellence. You can work quite successfully with competent native speakers or practical experts.

Many courses cover holidays or business in the language concerned and you don't necessarily need a qualified person for this, just a keen part-timer. One school offering French tuition employed a local French-born lady. Another offering Spanish used an English businessman who regularly visited Spain and enjoyed teaching his skill. Those you retain will probably work part-time and be paid per student. They will need to devise a suitable course made up of a number of lessons. Several educational publishers offer language tuition courses with complete text books and audio tapes. Advertise for tutors in the local press. Alternatively a school or college may have staff or students who could offer tuition.

Finally, find and book premises for the course. School premises are ideal if they have a language laboratory you can use. Otherwise, business customers might prefer a small hotel suite. A typical course might have 20 lessons over 20 weeks or weekends, a three- or four-day 9am – 6pm intensive course, which often appeals to business customers.

There is no limit to the languages you can offer — from one up to ten or so. French, German, Spanish, Italian (for business and holidays), Greek, Portuguese (mainly holidays), American English, Russian, Asian and African languages, Arabic, Chinese and Japanese are all possible, though in the more complex tongues you would probably cover only basic courtesies.

Sell your courses on their practical and specialist nature. Bear in mind that they will often appeal to business users — people who are in a hurry and rather than a complete introduction to the language want in-depth tuition on just the aspects that matter to them. It's often a good idea to offer a complete beginner's course and (for the more popular languages) an advanced course for those with some working knowledge.

Advertise the courses in the regional press, ideally in the business sections. You can also mail details to medium-sized businesses who might be involved in overseas trade. Have a prospectus outlining the course structure and content and enrolment details. Pricing depends on the nature of the course. It should reflect its specific nature and the fact that a course will take no more than four students to a tutor. A 20-lesson course could be priced at £300 – £800 per person, a four-day intensive course at £500. Take enrolments by post with a 25% deposit. State that the course commences within a month (or so) to give you time to fill it. There is no need to give an exact date and this will allow you time to advertise and sell it fully.

The selling and administration of the courses is the most difficult part. Once you have a tutor and students it is just a matter of bringing them together for lessons. One good sales point is to issue a Certificate of Competence to those whom the tutor feels could converse with a native speaker.

Opportunities for expanding the business from a simple start are many. Courses can be offered at different levels of ability and in many different languages or aspects of a language. Courses can be biased towards spoken or written work. Refresher courses for those converting from academic courses to practical speaking are popular. Apart from expanding the courses themselves, the sales effort can also be expanded. Many larger companies might consider paying for their entire workforce to learn the basics of a foreign language with which that business has some connection.

However you expand, keep the specialist nature of the course. This is the market niche you are aiming for, not the evening class and tape market.

## Summary

1. Provide specialist practical courses for businessmen and 'serious' holidaymakers.
2. Have no more than four students to a tutor, and charge a high fee.
3. Hold classes in a suitable place — a school language laboratory is ideal, but otherwise a hotel suite makes a good venue.
4. Take enrolments by post with a deposit of 25%.
5. It might be a good idea to issue a Certificate of Competence at the end of the course.

---

# PROJECT 96: A TRANSLATION SERVICE

| | |
|---|---|
| *Status* | Part-time, possibly full-time |
| *Capital required* | Moderate |
| *Return* | Moderate |

---

## In brief

**Project 95** is a valuable business service, but it is not the only service you can offer businessmen in the field of language. In larger cities there is scope to offer a foreign language business bureau.

With greater international co-operation there are plenty of opportunities to do business with foreign countries. In particular, relaxation of trading restrictions between European Economic Community members offers special scope. The major problem is always the language barrier. A service which overcomes that barrier could be greatly sought after.

Basically, you would recruit those experienced or qualified in foreign languages, then rent out their services as linguists helping businessmen dealing abroad. Your linguists could, for example, write introductory sales letters overseas, or prepare brochures in foreign languages. They could also help with negotiations over the telephone — and give an after-sales service in the language concerned. In short, you could enable businesses to expand in markets to which they previously had no access whatsoever.

Such a service is not particularly complex, but it does call for a certain degree of organisation between the various parties. Having said this it can be lucrative with fees to suit the figures that overseas deals can generate.

Proceed as with **Project 95**. The locating of reliable translators is vital before marketing the service.

# PROJECT 97: FANCY DRESS HIRE

| | |
|---|---|
| *Status* | Part-time, possibly full-time |
| *Capital required* | Moderate to high |
| *Return* | Moderate, long-term |
| *Can be combined with* | Projects 65, 80 and 90 |

## Project facts

Hiring out anything can be a good business. You get money for simply renting out something and the customer never owns it. One interesting variation of this is fancy dress hire. It is also a good business for home or small shop operation.

Fancy dress will never be a 'millionaire' type business, but there is definite scope, whether hiring for parties or theatrical purposes.

## What do I need?

- A spare room or small shop, an ideal business for a quieter area of a town or city with 'at the door' parking.
- Cash for costume making or purchase — minimum £500.
- Washing and repair facilities — could sub-contract.
- Consult the annual *British Theatre Directory* for background information. Also refer to periodicals such as *Drama* or *New Theatre Quarterly* (all available at main libraries).

## Pros and cons

| Pros | Cons |
|---|---|
| The same stock can make you money many times | Needs quite a lot of investment |
| Can eventually provide a steady income | Will take some time to establish |

## How do I operate

The basic requirement is the fancy dress costumes. These can be bought or made, depending on your resources. Go to theatrical suppliers and buy costumes. Alternatively look for the occasional theatrical auctions held when theatre productions end. Bargains are often found there. Costumes such as uniforms can often be bought at Government and other surplus sales. Alternatively you can have costumes made specially. Either do this yourself or look for a talented amateur seamstress locally. Patterns and fabrics are available from good fabric shops. Costumes can also be augmented with items from jumble sales at very low cost.

The exact type of costume you stock is up to you, but follow the usual fancy dress themes by looking at existing shops — the most popular are clowns, panto horses, exotic dancers, policemen etc. You can start with about 20 costumes (duplicate the popular ones), but 60 or 80 would be best.

This business will take time to establish. Making it a home operation is ideal. Some shops open in the evenings only, making part-time operation suitable. You can advertise in the press, but word of mouth is the best means of getting known. Much can be gained from good presentation, so ensure all costumes are on display if possible. Have fitting room facilities available.

Operate a booking scheme for costumes and hire them out by the day. Typical prices for a costume range from £8 to £20 a day, so even a new business hiring ten weekly makes a reasonable sideline. Established concerns could hire 50 or 60 a week.

Good maintenance is an important part of the business. Wash and repair costumes carefully after each hire, employing a local housewife if you like. Include cleaning in your price as it is better than leaving this to the customer. Apart from anything else, good presentation will get the repeat business vital in this concern.

You can expand by opening other branches, each sharing a 'library' of costumes; or you can open a rental 'shop within a shop', or offer the business as a franchise in other areas.

## Summary

1. Either buy or make the costumes, whichever you prefer.
2. The exact type of costume you stock is up to you, but follow the more popular themes initially.
3. You can operate from home or from a shop, but it is advisable to have parking.
4. You can advertise, but word of mouth is the best way of getting known.
5. Good maintenance of costumes is important. Arrange cleaning yourself, rather than asking the customers to do it.

## PROJECT 98: VENDING MACHINES

| | |
|---|---|
| *Status* | Mostly part-time |
| *Capital required* | Moderate to high |
| *Return* | Good, long-term |
| *Can be combined with* | Projects 5, 15, 23, and 93 |

### Project facts
One way of selling that doesn't involve actually selling is the vending machine. This also operates 24 hours a day, 7 days a week! Modern retailing has seen a growth in the use of vending machines and there are further opportunities for development. Establishing a vending round requires launch capital, but once established it needs little time and has few overheads. It can also attain a considerable resale value very quickly.

### What do I need?
- Capital for purchase of machines — minimum £500.
- Source of machines and stock.
- Sites to put the machines.
- The *Manufacturers and Merchants Directory* will have details of possible suppliers.
- The appropriate trade journal will give information on existing rounds, especially in confectionery and tobacco.

### Pros and cons

| Pros | Cons |
|---|---|
| Offers regular income for little work once established | May need considerable 'leg work' to get started |
| | The business demands regular time commitment |

### How do I operate?
First, do your market research. See what products are available from vending machines. See what types of products could be sold in this way. For example, sweets, drinks and tobacco are already available, but there is no reason why items like books, inexpensive jewellery or even ties and handkerchiefs (last minute gifts!) cannot be vended. Consider anything as long as it can be stored in, will last in, and can be dispensed by a machine.

Contact suppliers. A number of firms supply or make vending

machines. Look under **Vending Machine Manufacturers and Suppliers** in the Yellow Pages. Some will design new ones for your specific product. Ask for quotes from several suppliers. You will also need supplies. Machine suppliers can sometimes help. Check with manufacturers and wholesalers for suitable stock — whether chocolate or toys. Liaise between the machine supplier and the product supplier to ensure compatibility.

Sales sites will depend on the product and personal approaches to site owners are best. Shops, pubs and restaurants are ideal sites. Pay them a fixed monthly rent, or a share of takings. Plan a site indoors or outdoors depending on how weatherproof and vandal-proof the machines are. Also insure your machines.

Employ service agents. These are operatives with a van and a stock of supplies who visit each machine regularly to restock, collect the cash and clean the machine. (You may wish to do this yourself.)

Run a small sales office handling stock purchase, sales and machine takings, payments to landlords etc. Phase out unprofitable machines and capitalise on lucrative sites.

You can expand by adding new products or frequently updating equipment. Move into new areas or buy up and revitalise existing vending rounds. Alternatively, sell established rounds for good profits. Good resale value is a particular feature of this type of venture. For example, one good 25-machine confectionery round taking £550 a week recently sold for £25,000!

## How much can I earn?

The above confectionery round would typically take £550, which is, after all, only about 1,000 units of confectionery sold. The stock sold each week would cost around £320. Costs in servicing the round (eg transport) would cost about £25, with insurance and maintenance costing £40 on top of that. Total costs are therefore £385.

After all costs are paid this business would produce around £165 per week for four or five hours work, part time. Given the capital injection it wouldn't be impossible to operate six or seven of these rounds over an entire region.

## Summary
1. Research the market thoroughly to see what products could be sold in a vending machine.
2. Find a supplier of machines, and stock up on the items you want to sell. Liaise with the two suppliers, to ensure that the

machine is compatible with the stock.

3. Visit pubs, restaurants, clubs, shops or other locations to persuade them to rent you space for your machines. Either pay a rent or a share of the takings.

---

# PROJECT 99: PUBLIC CONVENIENCES

| | |
|---|---|
| *Status* | Full-time or sideline |
| *Capital required* | Very high |
| *Return* | Good, long-term |
| *Can be combined with* | Project 100 |

---

## Project facts
One interesting development recently has been the privatisation of facilities once offered by public authorities — including the privatisation of the public convenience. No longer need these facilities be inadequate council-owned concerns, but instead bright, clean commercial facilities which make their owners a great deal of money.

## What do I need?
- Considerable capital for building, if you can't lease existing facilities.
- A site.
- Attendants.

## Pros and cons

| Pros | Cons |
|---|---|
| Can be very lucrative | Needs a lot of capital |
| Very easy to run once built | Must be kept spotless and vandal-free to attract custom |

## How do I operate?
Decide on a site. This idea will only work in busy areas like city centres, airports, amusement parks or coastal areas. Identify possibilities in your region, using street plans.

Approach the local council. Ask if they would consider leasing you existing facilities. Some may consider this, others will not. If not you will have to build rival facilities on a spare plot of land. Large shopping centres, railway stations or airports may lease you some space.

Retain local builders and plumbers to design and build or

remodel the conveniences. Planning consent will be required for new facilities. You will need both ladies' and gents' facilities (also add a disabled WC). Equip all of them with modern fitments to a high standard.

Fit the entrance to the facilities with a coin-operated turnstile. The charge for entry to the unit for any purpose could range between 15p and 30p. You could also offer extra services like showers, hair dressing or left luggage at extra cost and fit vending machines for toothbrushes, razors and other personal services.

Employ attendants (male and female) to staff them throughout the opening hours of about 8am – 8pm. Their job will be to keep the premises spotless and ensure that people pay.

Open up your new enterprise and provide a first-class service. The concept is that people will pay for a good service in preference to free, sub-standard facilities. All existing evidence is that this succeeds.

## How much can I earn?

**Example:** Consider facilities in a busy city shopping centre. They attract 2,000 people daily from Monday to Friday, 3,500 on Saturday, each paying 20p. The income from this is £2,700 weekly. On top of this add an extra £600 from vending machines and other services, to total £3,300. This would be ample to pay staff costs, maintenance, water rates, loan repayments etc with a substantial profit margin on top.

## Summary
1. Find a site in a busy area.
2. Lease existing facilities if possible. If not, build your own.
3. Equip toilets to a high standard, and install vending machines for extra income.
4. Fit coin-operated turnstiles.
5. Employ attendants to keep them clean and ensure that everyone pays.

## PROJECT 100: OTHER COIN-OPERATED FACILITIES

| | |
|---|---|
| *Status* | Mostly part-time sidelines |
| *Capital required* | Mostly high |
| *Return* | Excellent, long-term |

### In brief

There is a great deal of scope in coin-operated facilities, because low staff costs can make previously uneconomical projects not only viable but extremely profitable. A number of services, old and new, are now available on coin-op, or even on a paper money operated basis. For example:

- A small gymnasium, equipped with coin operated exercise machines or accessible through a turnstile
- A hot spray car wash, vacuum and air for tyres at a service station (already exists but room to expand)
- Microcomputers, word processors and other office machines coin operated in an unmanned business services bureau
- A study room in cities for business people and students etc to use when away from their own offices
- 'Capsule' hotels in busy cities where a coin-op door gives use of a small sleeping cubicle for the night — suitable for business guests.

This concept can be extended to many different ideas. The main theme, though, is that a coin-op service is a service and much more than just a vending machine. Such services do need some capital outlay, some space, and an attendant on call for when things go wrong. But they do allow you to provide a range of business opportunities not practical in any other situation.

No standardised approach is possible. Such opportunities very much depend on spotting opportunities then planning and trying them yourself. The USA is a leader in these types of businesses. So a subscription to a US entrepreneurial magazine may be of great help. One magazine including such subjects is *Entrepreneur Magazine,* 2311 Pontius Avenue, Los Angeles, California, USA CA90064. Telephone from UK — 010 1 213 477 1011.

# PROJECT 101: LOTTERIES

| | |
|---|---|
| *Status* | Part-time, occasional |
| *Capital required* | High |
| *Return* | Very high, fast |
| *Can be combined with* | Projects 7 and 8 |

## Project facts

As an income booster lotteries and competitions might seem an attractive idea. However, few people see the *organisation* of lotteries as an effective way of making money. The truth is, though, that organising some sort of lottery has the potential to be a big money spinner within the constraints of the law.

Many companies use competitions as promotional devices, and of course, football pools are one of the most successful lottery-type operations. So there is scope to offer other people the chance to make money, while making it for yourself. It would also be possible to use this idea for a charity fund-raising event. Some cash is needed in this venture in order to get a much larger amount back, so it is ideal for a consortium of investors to work together.

## What do I need?

- Capital for prizes.
- An ability to sell.
- Legal advice is essential before you start.
- The Government department responsible for lotteries is the Home Office, 50 Queen Anne's Gate, London SW1H 9AT (Tel.01-213 3000). There is also the Gaming Board for Great Britain, 168–173 High Holborn, London, WC1V 7AA (Tel. 01-240 0821).

## Pros and cons

| Pros | Cons |
|---|---|
| Profits can be very large, very soon | Risk of loss if ticket sales fall short |
| | Must take care to avoid legal difficulties |

## How do I operate?

Before you start, retain a suitable solicitor to advise you on the legal aspects. Lottery regulations are quite complex and there are restrictions.

Decide on the size of the lottery — what kind of prize will be offered. This very much depends on the law and the capital available. One lottery offered a £40,000 house for a £5 ticket (and sold 20,000 tickets). Cars are popular lottery prizes. Five investors could buy a £5,000 car (putting up £1,000 each), then aim to sell 20,000 tickets at £1 each. Cash is popular too. You can start small though — perhaps offering an £800 holiday and selling 2,500 £1 tickets.

Have tickets and promotional posters printed. Use a specialist ticket printer. Look under **Printers** in the Yellow Pages. A good way to sell tickets is to appoint shops as sales agents. Pay a commission (say 10p on a £1 ticket). Better still, pay them in free tickets. Alternatively you could organise stands in town centres to sell — in much the same way as lottery tickets are already sold.

It's crucial to sell as many tickets as possible. If ticket sales are low a loss cannot be ruled out. For best results sell tickets to at least three times the value of the prize, ideally four times.

You will normally be committed to drawing the lottery on a certain date. Make something of an event of it — it's all publicity for the next lottery. Make a further ceremony of awarding the prize. Local press and TV may give coverage for even more publicity.

You can expand with regular lotteries, monthly (or even weekly), or with larger or multiple prizes to encourage more competitors. There is also potential to expand nationally according to legal limitations.

## Summary

1. It is essential to get legal advice, as lottery regulations are complex and limiting.
2. Decide what kind of prizes you are going to offer.
3. Have posters and tickets printed.
4. Appoint shops as sales agents, on a commission basis. You can also organise stands in town centres.
5. Make the draw and the presentation of prizes a big event, to gain the maximum publicity. This will help sales of future lotteries.

**General books**
Any library or major bookshop will offer several titles on the general mechanics of starting in business. The following titles may be of special interest.

*Working for Yourself* by Graham Rickard, Wayland (1984).
Interesting case histories of a number of self-employed people ranging from professionals to tradesmen to unskilled people starting in business.

*Work for Yourself* by Paddy Hall, National Extension College (1983).
A booklet intended for young people starting in business, but extremely helpful if you wish to start a project and know absolutely nothing about business!

*Working for Yourself*, a series of books on self-employment by various experienced and respected authors, published by Kogan Page.

*How to be Your Own Boss* by Conrad Frost, the Macmillan Press (1982).
Good general 'own-business' information with interesting and inspirational case histories.

*Croner's Reference Book for the Self-Employed and Smaller Business*, Croner Publications.
The leading reference guide on the routine and administration

of business. Includes all subjects from tax regulations to law. Updated monthly. Available direct from Croner's, 173 Kington Road, New Malden, Surrey KT3 3BE (Tel. 01-942 1188).

*How to Keep Business Accounts* by Peter Taylor, Northcote House Publishers (1988).
An easy-to-understand manual for the business owner which cuts right through the problems associated with 'doing the books'.

*How to Raise Business Finance* by Peter Ibbetson, Northcote House Publishers (1987).
A handbook giving the entrepreneur an insider's view of how to identify the kind of business finance needed, and where and how to obtain it.

*How to Start a Business from Home* by Graham Jones, Northcote House Publishers (1989).
A popular enterprise paperback giving all the details you need to get up and running in a business of your own. It shows how to profit from your own skills and experience from the comfort of your own home.

## Addresses
The following addresses may be useful for further contacts in business as a whole.

Small Firms Service, Department of Trade & Industry, Ashdown House, 127 Victoria Street, London SW1E 6RB. 01-212 8667.
Offers: Informative booklets, plus a counselling service which is initially free. Small Firms Centres can also be contacted on Freefone 2444. Local offices are at:

2–18 Ebury Bridge Road, London SW1W 8QD. 01-730 8451.
The Pithay, Bristol BS1 2NB. (0272) 294546.
Ladywood House, Stephenson Street, Birmingham BS1 2NB. 021-643 3344.
16 St David's House, Wood Street, Cardiff CF1 1ER. (0222) 396116.
Carlyle House, Carlyle Road, Cambridge CB4 3DN. (0223) 63312.
120 Bothwell Street, Glasgow G2 7JP. 041-248 6014.
Graeme House, Derby Square, Liverpool L2 7UJ. 051-236 5756.
1 Park Row, Leeds LS1 5NR. (0532) 445151.
3 Cloth Market, Newcastle NE1 3EE. 091-232 5353.
Royal Exchange Buildings, St Anne's Square, Manchester M2 7AH. 061-832 5282.
20 Middle Pavement, Nottingham NG1 7DW. (0602) 581205.

Abbey Square, Reading RG1 3BE. (0734) 591733.

In Northern Ireland contact:
Industrial Development Board for Northern Ireland, IDB House, 64 Chichester Street, Belfast BT1 4JX. (0232) 233233.

National Federation of Self Employed and Small Businesses, 32 St. Anne's Road, Lytham St. Annes, Lancs FY8 1NY. (0253) 720911.
Also at: 45 Russell Square, London WC1 4JF. 01-636 3828.

Alliance of Small Firms and Self-Employed People, 42 Vine Road, East Molesey, Surrey KT8 9LF. 01-979 2293.

Business in the Community, 227 City Road, London EC1V 1JU. 01-253 3716.
Offers details on local enterprise agencies.

The Institute of Small Business, 1 Whitehall Square, London SW1A 2HD. 01-839 7645.

COSIRA (Council for Small Industries in Rural Areas), 141 Castle Street, Salisbury, Wilts SP1 3TP. (0722) 336255.
Offers help and contacts for rural businesses.

Small Business Bureau, 32 Smith Square, London WC1P 3HA. 01-222 9000.

The Marketing Guild, 482 Dunstable Road, Luton, Bedfordshire LU4 8DL. (0582) 490441.
Offers regular newsletter on marketing technique.

Office of Fair Trading, Field House, Breams Buildings, London EC4A 1PR. 01-242 2858.
Offers information on consumer rights and some licences.

The Advertising Standards Authority, Brook House, Torrington Place, London WC1E 7HN.
Offers information on advertising regulations and codes of practice. This is of help if you are organising your own advertising.

Companies Registration Office, Crown Way, Maindy, Cardiff CF4 3UZ. (0222) 388588.
Offers company registration and advice on business names.

COI (Central Office of Information), Hercules Road, Westminster Bridge Road, London SE1 7DU. 01-298 2345.
Offers some Government information publications.

Inland Revenue, Somerset House, London WC2R 1LB. 01-438 6622.
Also refer to your local office listed in the telephone directory.

HM Customs & Excise, King's Beam House, Mark Lane, London EC3R 7HE. 01-626 1515.
Also refer to your local office listed in the telephone directory.

Department of the Environment, 2 Marsham Street, London SW1P 3EB. 01-212 3434.
The ultimate authority on planning matters.

Department of Employment, Caxton House, Tothill Street, London SW1H 9NF. 01-213 5551.
Offers information on Government schemes.

Her Majesty's Stationery Office, St Crispins, Duke Street, Norwich NR3 1PD. (0603) 622211.
Publishes Government books, many explaining regulations, policy etc in easy-to-understand language. Consult the Annual Catalogue of HMSO Books at libraries.

Training Commission, Moorfoot, Sheffield S1 4PQ.(0742) 753275.
Contact local offices via Job Centres. Offers training schemes and some business finance schemes.

Department of Social Security, Alexander Fleming House, London SE1 6BY. 01-407 5522.

The Post Office, 33 Grosvenor Place, London SW1X 1PX. 01-235 8000.

The Law Society, 113 Chancery Lane, London WC2. 01-242 1222.

British Insurance Brokers Association (BIBA), Fountain House, Fenchurch Street, London EC3M 5DJ. 01-623 9043.

Institute of Chartered Accountants, PO Box 433, Moorgate Place, London EC2P 2BJ.

British Franchise Association, 75a Bell Street, Henley On Thames, Oxon RG9 2BD.
Offers information on franchise business opportunities.

**Local contacts**
You should always look for local sources of business help. Frequently these are tailored to business conditions in your area and so are of great practical help.

The local library usually has a register of local trade societies, associations or clubs.

The local council will have details of Development or Enterprise Agencies operating locally. These agencies are funded by local authorities and existing businesses and can offer practical aid and sometimes finance.

Citizens Advice Bureaux, provide various useful contacts. They might be able to suggest solicitors, accountants etc who will help start-up business people.

The local telephone directory and Yellow Pages are good sources of trade contacts and other information.